ZEENA SHAH

marbling

Projects, Design Ideas + Techniques for a More Colourful Life

Photography by Kristin Perers

Hardie Grant

QUADRILLE

Introduction

I remember the first time my Mum bought me a craft kit. It was a DIY pompom dog kit and naturally I was ecstatic, conscientiously wrapping my brown yarn around various circular cardboard templates to create my fluffy dog. I must have been 6 or 7 years old and she had recently taught me how to knit and basket weave, among other crafts. Little did I know she'd inspire a lifelong love of making things, and years later a career to boot. I do still love a pompom and am patiently awaiting the real dog one day!

I trained as a textile designer at Chelsea School of Art and immediately fell in love with surface pattern design. I'd spend most of my time in the print room, with the dye lab next door a close second, garnering as much know-how as I could from our wonderful technician, Margaret.

The immediacy of screen printing became an addiction of sorts. I'd spend hours weighing out tiny measures of powder dyes, mixing up colours and sampling them on various fabrics so I had just the right colour combination. It really was a labour of love. There were plenty of dye disasters and smudged prints as I found my way, but there is so much joy in the printmaking process and being quite meticulous, it suited me and I learnt to love the mess. My first book *How To Print Fabric* was just the beginning of sharing my creative journey into surface pattern design and I'm so excited to be able to share my next chapter, on marbling, with you.

I've spent the last twelve years working as a textile designer, illustrator, studio assistant, teacher, art director, stylist, prop maker, content creator, writer and more recently presenter, spreading my love of craft and creativity. You tend to become very good at spinning lots of plates as a creative person (partly as it is often the only way to make ends meet as a freelancer) and as my career progressed I realised that

I am just one of those people that thrives on the variety of life and lives for learning new skills and creating things with my hands. It's not been an easy journey but I'm so lucky to have found my passion in life and am making it my mission to spread the creativity bug in everything that I do; it is contagious.

Marbling draws on my passion for surface pattern design and was a natural exploration for me as a print designer. Nature is filled with limitless inspiration and this age-old beautiful technique is one that can mesmerise with endless possibilities because there is an infinity of patterns to be made using this single technique. It really is quite magical. Like screen printing, its simplicity and immediacy brought me such joy and I'd found my new crafty addiction.

When the pandemic first hit and we were plunged into uncertainty and a new normal, I began sharing short crafty tutorials over on my Instagram account, @heartzeena, hoping to inspire some joyful creativity from behind my phone screen. Before I knew it, I'd found a community of like-minded colour lovers in which I could spark creativity and encourage to make things from home using everyday objects. I helped them find joy and a new creative confidence in making things.

In our increasingly busy and often all-consuming digital first lives, taking some time out for 'Mindful Marbling' became a way to slow down and lose yourself in craft. I'm still blown away by the ability of technology to connect and reach so many. It's incredible really, but after a while there's only so much mindless scrolling you can do and like all crafts, marbling is a wonderful way to switch off, enjoy some 'you' time and escape reality, even if just for a short time. You can get lost in the mesmerising world of ink and water manipulation so easily and often I find myself just swirling away the ups and downs of life in the way I use inks in the marbling water bath, because it is so therapeutic.

Marbling has been around for centuries and I want to bring this precious technique back to the modern day – it's not just for bookbinding endpapers and paper, there is so much you can do with this incredible craft. In this book I'll show you how you can transform everyday objects, textiles, paper and materials destined for the bin into marbled treasures that will bring colour, joy and life to you and your home spaces inexpensively. I am self taught and by no means an expert but am a firm believer that everyone can be creative. All you have to do is find your creative confidence and in this book I hope to encourage you to find yours and have fun with colour using this truly magical and rather addictive technique.

Come with me and experience modern marbling my way!

A Brief History of Marbling

Marbling is pretty old school: the craft dates back to the 12th century – it was first referenced to have been practiced by artisans in Japan. That said, it is likely to have originated much earlier than this because the techniques were kept very secretive and so it is very difficult to trace the craft's true origins since it was rarely documented. The secrecy around the technique makes it even more of an exciting and intriguing craft, as well as one I was desperate to have a go at the minute I realised its magic!

The art of marbling has since been spotted all over the world. It is most well known in Italy, as well as in Persia, Turkey, India and a number of other countries in its various papery forms. The skill and its secrets were thought to have travelled via the trading routes and evolved over the years; the techniques differ ever so slightly from country to country and artisan to artisan, but the effects are very similar and utterly mesmerising. Marbling was first practiced in the UK in the 17th century but it is on the red list of endangered crafts today, which is even more reason to bring this brilliant craft back to life in a modern and accessible way.

Marbling is a method of aqueous surface pattern design that mimics its natural stone counterpart. Its magic comes from its uniqueness. No design is the same due to the nature of the technique – which is what I love so much about the artform. It is much like nature in this way. The organic nature of the patterns it creates is also so pleasing to the eye, which I'm sure adds to its addictive quality. Paint or ink is floated on the surface of a water bath, then there are many different techniques that can be used. In the Japanese technique known as Suminagashi, which means 'floating ink', the ink is carefully painted onto the water to create patterns that are then transferred onto Japanese washi or rice papers by dipping them into the water bath.

In the Turkish method 'Ebru', meaning 'a cloud', the water is treated with size and ink is then carefully dropped into the water bath using traditional brushes and a stylus. The paper is then placed into the water bath, submerged and removed to reveal the pattern. This is most similar to the techniques you might have seen at work today and those we'll be using in this book.

Traditionally the papers created would have been used in the bookbinding process as book covers or endpapers – those exquisite marbled endpapers that you might have come across in old books and stationery; well, that's what

marbling was most commonly crafted for. Its uniqueness added to its high-end luxurious feel and meant it was very desirable for these types of works – and it was impossible to imitate so it was often used for important or official government documents, too – and sometimes in extravagant interiors.

These days the techniques are still very similar to those used throughout history, but fewer marbling artists exist than in the past because the craft itself can be very involved and time-consuming. Whilst the process of manipulating ink onto water looks simple it requires a huge amount of skill to perfect, so marbling was therefore less appealing for commercial projects. Also, with the speed of the digital world, hand-crafting a marbled design will never be as efficient as Photoshop! That said, marbling is making a huge comeback. The craft has been growing in popularity over the past decade as consumers question how things are made and place more value on traditional craftsmanship. This intriguing and unique craft really does have a special place, and there are currently quite a few marbling artists and studios around the world giving this magical technique a much-deserved resurgence. After all, there is nothing more satisfying than making something with

your hands – and this is a hand craft that should be celebrated, because the results you can achieve with the simple motion of moving ink through water are quite spectacular.

As marbling grows in popularity once again, it's by no means an old-school craft anymore. It has been spotted on catwalks during fashion weeks, in modern stationery collections, and adorning luxury packaging and designer homeware, so it's the perfect addition to our modern creative and conscious lifestyles. There are now endless possibilities for marbling with the types of ready-mixed inks and colours available today, so this once laborious technique can now be surprisingly speedy. I love being able to whip up a marbled greetings card and matching gift wrap the night before a birthday. Marbling also lends itself brilliantly to upcycling; one of my favourite ways to give an empty glass candle pot or glass drinks bottle a second life is to marble it and turn it into a vase, plant pot or pen holder. In a waste-conscious world I am always trying to craft more mindfully, so to be able to give objects that might be thrown into landfill a second life is a crafty win in my book. But to be very honest it's also just incredibly fun, so I am excited to share how you can bring it into your life in a modern way!

How to Use This Book

This section covers the materials you will need, how to work with colour, and details some of the basic marbling techniques used in the book.

Materials are really important; you can achieve different looks depending on what type of inks you choose. I firmly believe craft shouldn't be costly or too time-consuming and I aim to make it as accessible and sustainable as I can, so the projects use a variety of everyday objects, challenging your upcycling skills – and you'll be amazed at what you can do with nail polish. I want you to read this book and get started straight away from your kitchen table. I also combine this magical technique with other crafts to create meaningful objects for your home.

Colour is a big part of the marbling process and intrinsically linked to our mood. I want to inspire you to live a more colourful and creative life by embracing your creativity and finding your colour confidence. It's by far a more joyful way of living! In this section I explore what colour evokes, what kind of feelings, and how this can relate to your work and the way you think about your colour choices. For me, choosing my colour palette is one of the most inspiring parts of the design process. It's something I have always been drawn to, from the hours I spent in the dye lab at art school to choosing the colour of our wedding stationery – or even how I go about colour blocking in my outfit of the day or choosing a throw for the sofa. You'll hone your eye for colour by carefully considering how to work with it in the marbling process and beyond.

The process of marbling itself is a simple one; once you've mastered the basic techniques, practise and experimentation are key. Rather than focusing on the end result, the joy of the marbling process is about getting comfortable with making a mess, being open to getting it wrong (it's all part of the journey) and playing with the technique. Like most crafts, the more you do it the better you will get and with every print comes more experience. So leave your inner perfectionist at the door, because in this book you will embrace your creative identity and bring personality to your work though your colour choices and pattern making. The joy and true beauty of marbling is in each unique pattern and this all comes from you and every mark you make, ink spot you drop and colour you choose.

So let's get started!

Things You Will Need

I want to make getting creative with marbling as easy as possible, so here are some things you will need to get started right away.

One of the best things about marbling my way is that you won't need to invest in lots of expensive materials and equipment. The idea is that you'll be able to read this book and have a go at your kitchen table the very same day, using materials like nail polish that you might already have at home. In a world where waste and sustainability are always in the front of our minds I want to encourage a more conscious way of crafting wherever possible – and as this technique lends itself so beautifully to upcycling there will be some suggestions throughout the projects of things to which you could give a second life.

The techniques that I share in this book vary based on time, effort and skill needed. They start with simple and speedy nail-polish marbling and move onto the more traditional time-consuming Ebru marbling method as your confidence grows. Just head to the techniques section on pages 26–49 to learn about the processes in more detail.

Once you've mastered the techniques I guarantee you'll be marbling everything in sight and can pick and choose each method and material based on the project in mind.

Marbling bath

A shallow metal tray that can be filled with water to a depth of about 2.5cm (1in), just larger than A4 in size, will work well for a range of projects. I'd also recommend having a smaller tray for sampling work. I often use a roasting tray/disposable foil tray – or vegetables from the supermarket often come in a perfect-sized plastic tray that can be reused for marbling. Make sure to set aside trays just for marbling as some inks are solvent-based so you wouldn't want to use them for cooking by mistake.

You will also need a deeper dish or bowl for some of the projects where you will be marbling a larger object. See the projects for any specific requirements.

Water

Plenty of room-temperature, distilled water works best, but you can also use tap water brought to room temperature. The water temperature can really make a difference to the way the marbling inks hit and disperse on the surface of the water. You'll need enough to fill your water bath two-thirds of the way full.

Gloves

Marbling is a messy business so have some disposable silicone-free gloves handy for all of your projects. Change them regularly to avoid marking materials yet to be marbled. Biodegradable gloves are readily available online now, too.

Table cover and cleaning cloth

It's a good idea to cover the surface you'll be marbling onto as the ink may splash onto surfaces it shouldn't do, and also keep a cleaning cloth handy.

Clothing

Don't wear your best clothes for marbling as ink may splash as you drop it into the water bath, or when you move it to create patterns. An apron is always handy.

Inks

We'll be exploring four marbling techniques in this book and for each you need the following:

Nail-polish marbling

Different shades of regular nail polish, the newer the polish the better the effect. Start with two or three colours and add more as you master the process. It's best used on paper or card.

Ready-mixed marbling inks

These are readily available online and in art shops; they may come in a marbling kit (see page 138 for some of my favourite suppliers) or be sold as individual inks. My personal preference and the inks I use most regularly in this book are **Marabu Easy Marble inks**. They're solvent-based, which means they're great for ceramics, wood and glass surfaces. For paper-based marbling, a basic paper marbling kit will work perfectly.

Marbling with size

The third technique uses size to thicken the water of the marbling bath, which can then be used with acrylic, gouache or watercolour paints. This allows much more flexibility and precision with colour and more intricate pattern creation.

Carragheen or Irish moss is the most popular size used historically, and by modern marblers. You can buy it in a powder form called **carrageenan** to blend with water so the inks sit on top rather than float to the bottom of the bath. Make sure you choose the lambda grade, which is the only variety you can use as a marbling size. I found it easily online but there are other varieties that create a more gel-like substance that won't work for marbling. I love that it is a natural product from the sea.

You can also use **Methocel** size, which is less expensive and a little easier to find. It can be mixed with water in the same way as carrageenan but may affect the inks differently so it's worth sampling a small amount first. We'll be using carrageenan size in this book.

You'll need a **spoon**, **measuring scale** or **jug/ cup**, a **whisk** and a **blender** to mix the size with water.

Acrylic paints in a selection of colours; I recommend Liquitex or Golden brands for excellent colour intensity. I use them for multiple craft projects and find acrylics easiest to work with when getting to grips with this technique.

Ox gall or **Kodak Photo-Flo** is used to dilute and disperse the acrylic paints so they can be used in the size.

Alum (Aluminium potassium sulphate) is a mordant used to treat paper and fabrics before marbling. It can also be found online easily. Apply with a **natural sponge** before marbling following the manufacturer's instructions.

Once you've mastered working with acrylics and size, you can experiment with gouache, oil or watercolour paints using the same methods.

Suminagashi

This technique calls for Japanese pigment inks known as **sumi inks**. These traditional inks are made using pine wood ash so the ink is brighter and more crisp than Indian ink. I use the **Boku-Undo** variety as it comes in a few different colours as well as black. **Indian ink** also works with this technique, but will be less vibrant.

You'll need **sumi** or **calligraphy brushes**, **jars** or a **palette** to hold inks, and **Kodak Photo-Flo** as a surfactant – **washing-up liquid** (dish soap) will also work.

Paper

When choosing paper for marbling onto I recommend experimenting with a variety of weights. Lighter papers like 80gsm printer paper are easy to manipulate but saturate faster than heavier types. Paper and card from 80gsm to 350gsm is ideal; anything heavier will prove difficult to manipulate in water, which may lead to a gap in your print. I save up packaging scraps for marbling as it's a good way to use up your waste. You'll also need newspaper or newsprint strips to clean and skim the marbling bath.

Waste bin

Keep this close by your marbling bath for any newspaper skimming scraps.

Fabric

Natural fabrics will always work best for any kind of dye transfer project. The projects in this book use **silk habotai**, **100% linen** and **cotton lengths** because they take colour really well and have a beautiful finish. You can find these fabrics easily in a haberdashery or online. Pieces will need to be of a size to fit comfortably inside the marbling bath to print fully.

Stylus

You can use any pointed object as a stylus to manipulate the ink in your water bath. I use cocktail sticks (toothpicks), wooden skewers, paintbrushes of all shapes and sizes, T-pins, plastic combs – or you can find similar tools used in pottery (called needle tools) in art shops or online. You can get creative here; many marbling artists make their own whisks using the straw bristles cut from a broom and tied together with an elastic band to drop ink into their size, or make their own comb using balsa wood and T-pins.

Drying tools

Creating a space to lay wet marbled papers is essential to ensure a smooth marbling production process. Lay out a **plastic sheet** for paper to dry on, or hang fabrics and larger sheets of paper on a **drying rack** to drip dry. You might also want a couple of **dowel rods** to lift paper and fabric out of the marbling bath.

Jars and pipettes

Collect up any old glass jars and pots for mixing inks. As you advance I also recommend getting some pipettes, which you can pick up from your local craft shop or online, to allow more precision when dropping ink into the marbling bath. They come in all different shapes and sizes; start small as a little ink goes a long way.

Clear matt varnish

This may come in spray form or it can be painted on with a paintbrush. It will protect any delicate marbled surfaces.

Finding Your Colour Confidence

As a huge colour enthusiast, working with colour is one of the most inspiring parts of the design process for me. Your colour choices when marbling can make or break a design, so it is well worth considering your colour palette carefully in advance to avoid a mindblank or disappointment halfway through the process. You don't want your inks to become a mess of dingy browns (which is what always happened to me if I got too excited with poster paints as a child). Instead we're looking for sophisticated sepia!

As a colour fiend it's often easy to forget how difficult it can be to know where to start with colour. It can feel daunting and a bit scary, so I'm going to share some tips and tricks that have helped me along the way and will guide you so you know where to begin. And slowly, over time, you will find your colour confidence, too.

I've been teaching craft workshops for a number of years now and often, when I'm teaching a printmaking class or running a mindful marbling workshop, I'll be asked what colours to start with and what makes a good colour combination. The answer is that there are no wrong answers and no two right colours to begin with, because we all see colour in our own way. But there are certainly colour combinations that are more aesthetically pleasing to the eye than others.

Taking time to understand the basics of colour theory and how colours work together is a great place to begin your colour journey and a good way to help inform your colour choices. It will help to answer these questions, so the next time you grab your paints or inks you'll have a palette in mind and know exactly what to expect.

Of course part of the joy of marbling is in the happy accident, so don't feel you have to be too rigid with colour. However, I'd always recommend testing your chosen colours first to see how they behave and work together in water and on the surface they'll be covering (this is known as sampling, more on it later). So once you've mastered the techniques, spend some time sampling different colourways and materials to create your dream patterns and develop your skills. You'll then be well on your way to colour confidence!

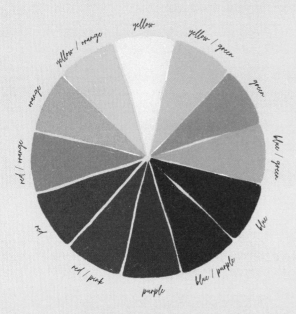

The colour wheel labels (clockwise from top): yellow, yellow / green, green, blue / green, blue, blue / purple, purple, red / pink, red, red / orange, orange, yellow / orange

There are three groups of colours within the colour wheel:

Primary colours: Red, Yellow, Blue

Secondary colours: Green, Orange, Violet

The colour wheel

Let's start with the colour wheel, first created by Sir Isaac Newton following his detailed studies of white light reflected through a prism. He discovered this created the colours we see and know today as those in the colour wheel and in one of my favourites, the rainbow. This is always my go-to for colour inspiration.

The colour wheel is a great tool to use as an artist and designer when developing a colour palette, because you can quickly and easily see the relationships between the colours. It also reminds me of the ones I've forgotten about, so I'd always recommend starting here if you're feeling uncertain. Knowing these basic groups of colours will also help you with understanding how to put colour together. This is integral to marbling because you're more often than not working with two to five colours at a time.

Tertiary colours: These colours are created by mixing the primary and secondary colours together, so Red-Orange, Yellow-Orange, Yellow-Green, Blue-Green, Blue-Violet, Red-Violet

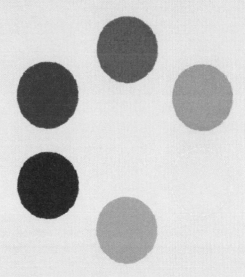

You can then add Black or White, or both mixed as Grey, to any of these colours to change the shade, tint and tone. Adding Black will alter the 'shade', adding White will alter the 'tint', while adding Grey will alter the 'tone.'

Starting with a set of primary and secondary colours will give you plenty of colours to begin building a palette. Have a go at mixing up and painting your own colour wheel; keep it on your fridge or workspace wall so it's always there for reference if you are suddenly lost for inspiration. It's also a helpful reminder of the colours you might have forgotten about – humans are creatures of habit and if you're like me you'll be drawn back to the same two colours, so make sure you challenge yourself and get out of that colour comfort zone. I like to set a new colour theme or palette per project to encourage me to get out of my mine! You could work your way through each colour of the rainbow for example, which would be a great way to start experimenting with ink colours.

As your colour confidence grows, experiment with two or three colours at a time – but no more than six because it can be difficult to distinguish patterns and work well with too many colours in the mix. It also helps to limit your choices since there are so many dreamy colours to choose from.

Complementary colours

These sit opposite each other on the colour wheel. This is one of my go-to colour formulas for a palette and I find using two complementary colours works really well in marbling. Some of my favourite colour combinations are:

Green + Pink
Orange + Blue
Red + Green

See below:

Triadic colours

These colours are equidistant from each other on the colour wheel – so they might be Red, Yellow and Blue, for example.

Analogous colours

These are three colours that sit next to each other on the colour wheel – so Red, Red-Violet and Violet will work harmoniously.

The joy of the marbling process is getting comfortable with colour and finding your way with the palette you choose, which will then inform your design.

Don't be afraid to add Black or White to give your palette some contrast. Often a splash of Black can really make a design pop and give it some depth if it feels a bit flat.

For a more sophisticated and sensitive palette, try working with just one colour and varying the shade, tone and tint by adding varying combinations of Black and White. This is often seen in the Japanese Suminagashi patterns, which always feel very calming and serene due to the nature of their softer ink tones.

Most importantly, have fun! If it starts to feel stressful or overwhelming, take a break and come back to your colour wheel with fresh eyes. Colour can easily overwhelm because there is so much choice, which can be less helpful than you might think. Don't feel defeated if you feel like this, it's just time for a cuppa and a biscuit.

Colour therapy

Colour is intrinsically linked to mood and colour therapy plays a huge part in my life on a daily basis. Colour therapy or chromatherapy is an alternative psychotherapy, in which colour and light are used to boost mood and wellbeing. You may have heard of Seasonal Affective Disorder (also called Winter depression or SAD), which is a seasonal depression that correlates with a lack of light. It is often treated with bright light and colour therapy.

Before I even knew what colour therapy was I was practising it. Wearing bright yellow will bring me immediate joy, much like a burst of sunshine. A grey jumper will feel less energising than a bright red or vibrant green, whilst blue is a much more calm and reflective colour and often linked with a good night's sleep. I am always in a positive and more joyful mood when wearing something pink and strongly believe pink is a neutral! What I love about colour is that it is infectious; not only does it make you feel good, it also makes those around you smile. Being self aware and noticing how colour makes you feel can be a game changer for embracing a life filled with more colour and finding your colour confidence.

Start to notice how certain colours make you feel. If you have a favourite colour; why do you think this is – is it because of a certain feeling or memory it evokes? Note down which colours bring about different emotions. Beginning to notice the way you behave around colour will inform your colour choices and is a brilliant source of inspiration for your work – and everyday life, too. Life is far too short not to live in colour, and when the benefits are so positive it's a no brainer.

Inspiration and where to find it

Colour inspiration is everywhere. You can start training your eye for colour by making notes and collecting colour ideas that you spot in everyday life. For me, nature is a great source of colour inspiration – as well as just getting dressed, people watching or reading a magazine. I am always taking photos of inspiring and pleasing colour palettes. I also love looking at interiors and old movies for memorable colour palettes, it's one of my favourite places to start a project. I am old fashioned so I love leafing through magazines and tearing out inspirational images to collect in my sketchbook. Pinterest is also a brilliant resource for colour because there are thousands and thousands of palettes on there that you can pin to unique digital moodboards.

Take photos or screenshot and print out what catches your eye, which you can then match a palette to. Keep such photos in your sketchbook and make notes about why they interest you and why they bring you joy. What is it that you love about them? Your sketchbook is an invaluable tool to gather inspiration – it should feel like your creative BFF! Use your walls, too, or even your fridge. Pin inspiration up next to your colour wheel and change it up regularly. Not all of us have the luxury of a dedicated creative space so I love using the 'save' tool on Instagram to create boards there, too. It's always a reach away on my mobile phone and a constructive use of my scroll time.

Pantone swatch books are another of my go-tos; having worked with colour as a textile designer I would pull out the tiny paper colour swatches and play around with them to build my colour palettes. The Pantone books can be pretty costly (although often you can bag a bargain on eBay secondhand) so why not create your own by painting out swatches of colour onto paper that can then be cut out – or nab some paint colour cards from your local DIY store and save those for inspiration.

Your colour palette might also be informed by the project and where or what it is for. For example, if it's a cushion for your home it might be that you choose some contrasting colours or go for similar tones. The world is your colourful oyster and it is full of inspiration.

Sampling how tos

Sample, sample, sample! This is definitely one of the things I learnt early on at art school. Sampling can sometimes feel rather laborious and time consuming (especially when you'd rather just get on with it) but is actually the key to refining your design colour palette and marbling practice.

I love to create a little sketchbook for each project that I'm working on. Either grab a ready-made sketchbook or make one yourself using scrap paper, a hole punch and a couple of binding screws or string; it needn't be fancy, just a home for the notes and swatches from all your colour tests. Start with your chosen materials and cut out some small pieces to create swatches. I always start with paper because this is the least expensive material and the easiest surface to marble onto. Take notes and jot down the colours you're using, quantities, and any specific brushes and paper types. Note down how each reacts with the marbling inks. Once your swatch is dry, attach it to your sketchbook with its corresponding notes.

Let's go back to our colour wheel: begin with the primary, secondary and tertiary colours and you'll soon realise there are so many colours to play with. One of the hardest parts of working with colour is editing your favourites down to a simple palette of two to five colours. This takes time, skill and experience, which will all come from the sampling process.

Once you're happy with your palettes, I would pull them out of your sketchbook and pin them to the wall, or keep them close by when marbling, to ensure you will get the results that you want.

Experimentation

Once you've chosen a colour palette to work with (I'd recommend two to three colours to begin with) you've done the hard work so onto the fun bit! Have fun and experiment with the colour using the colour wheel fundamentals and your eye for colour. It's time to play!

Work in small quantities – less is always more, especially when working with colour. You can always add more but once you've gone all in you will likely have to start again.

Don't forget about white and black; play with the tone, tint and shade for each colour to really understand what the outcome will be.

Once you've experimented and mixed up all of these colourways you should have plenty of swatches from which you can edit your palette down again.

Don't forget to make notes on exactly which colours you're using and how much.

I love using glass jars and pipettes so I can note down how many drops of colour I use every time. There are definitely occasions where I am less precise, but it's a good challenge to start out being technical – as with baking, there's a bit of a science to it.

Colour block

OK, so things don't always go to plan, especially when working with a new and messy craft, so you've got a colour block. It is much more common than you might think!

My best advice for managing a colour block is to take a break. Remember that it is totally normal to get a little overwhelmed with colour – there are so many options and combinations. Step away from your marbling zone and get some air, go for a walk or come back to your craft another day. You don't have to conquer colour in one session, finding your colour confidence is a journey and the more you work with colour the better your eye will be. When you return with fresh eyes you'll realise it's easily resolved and start again. Keep making notes in your sketchbook to refer back to the next time this happens and it might inspire something completely new. Don't forget that any craft takes time to get right and the more you practise the better you will be. So don't worry about the disasters; we all have them and they're part of the process.

I like to jot down my favourite 'colour wins' so that I can quickly head to that page if I'm feeling stuck. They might be a snap of a project that went really well or just a swatch of a few colours I loved together. It's always good to celebrate the wins.

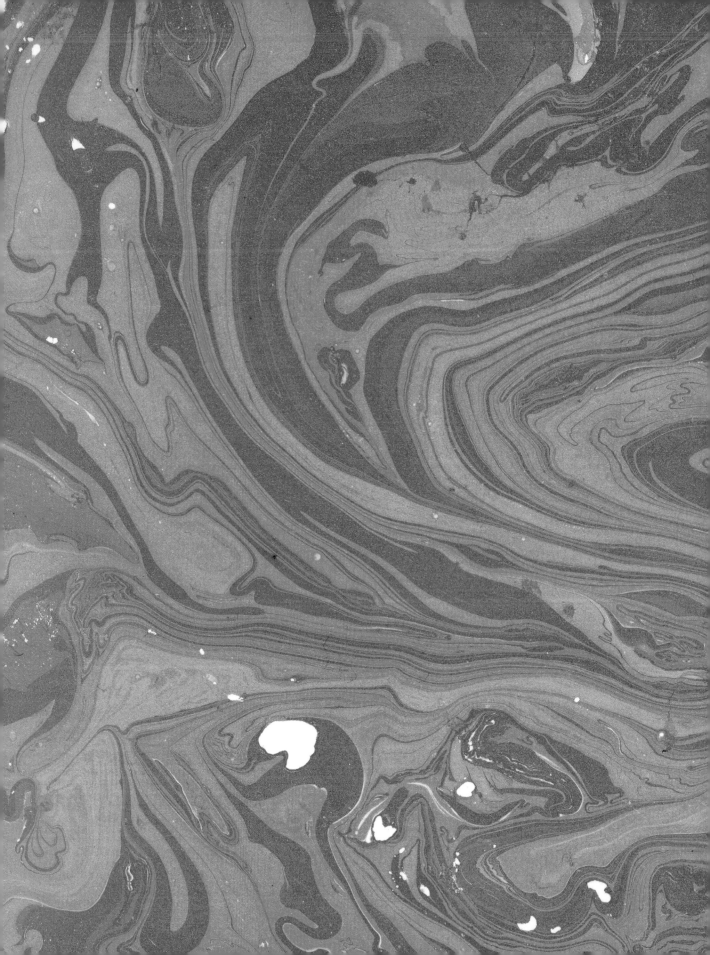

In this chapter you'll discover four key marbling techniques to explore, which will bring this once very secretive process into the modern day in a new, accessible and colourful way. You'll be marbling everything in sight before you know it!

techniques

The traditional methods of marbling really haven't changed much since the 17th century, when they first arrived in the UK. The biggest difference now is that we are spoilt for choice, with an array of different products that can be used to create a modern marbled surface pattern.

The more I research and practise marbling, trying the many varieties of pre-mixed inks and kits available, the more I realise the techniques vary from artist to artist as much as from product to product. There is no one right way to marble so I encourage you to give each method here a try to work out which one works best for you and your marbling practice. Remember this is just the beginning of your marbling journey! This section covers four key techniques for marbling, starting with the simplest and ending with the more traditional. These are my most used and by far my favourite techniques for marbling. They are also the ones I feel are the most useful and accessible to the modern crafter. Often a new craft can feel a little daunting so there's something for everyone here, no matter what their skill level. Then once you're familiar with all the techniques you'll be able to pick and choose the one to suit your project.

I'd recommend planning your projects in advance because the more traditional size marbling technique is a little more of a process and much more time consuming than the other techniques. I encourage you to set aside plenty of time to get to grips with it, experiment and enjoy the happy accidents as they happen.

Preparation

Marbling can be messy (the joy is in the mess making, trust me!) so before you begin cover your surface with a wipe-clean table cover. Have a cloth and bin nearby for any disasters and paper waste. Wear clothing you don't mind getting paint on and always wear gloves when using solvent-based products or working with alum.

When marbling surfaces that aren't paper-based, use a lint-free cloth and rubbing alcohol to remove any dust or residue as this will affect your marbling inks. Often one of the reasons my ink does not take to a surface is because the object isn't 100% clean. Even our hands can leave oils on the surface of an object and affect a print. Making sure your space is free of dust and lint is also important because if particles fall into the water bath they will affect your print. I love these little details but if you are a perfectionist you might want to go all out on the cleaning front – although I recommend you fall in love with these little imperfections too.

When using solvent-based products keep windows open and always work in a well-ventilated space.

The water bath

With all these marbling techniques you will begin by making what is known as a marbling bath, as in the Ebru method of marbling. This is simply a tray at least 2.5cm (1in) deep filled with distilled room-temperature water. The object to be marbled should fit inside comfortably. See page 16 for more information on marbling baths.

Notes on the techniques

This might all feel like a lot of information but as you work through each technique you will notice that they aren't too dissimilar from one another. No matter where the techniques originated, as they travelled from country to country each borrowed from the others. Use this section to pick and choose the technique that works best for you, the time you have available, and what you would like to marble. There is something for everyone, no matter what their skill level.

Marbling is a process and experimenting with these techniques is the first step on your journey. It takes years and years to perfect. But remember to have fun and enjoy the magic and mindfulness it can bring. Don't worry too much about the disasters along the way. Trust me, there will be many but persistence is fruitful and the end results will have you wanting to marble everything in sight, no matter what goes wrong.

If you are finding something tricky head to the troubleshooting section on page 140; there may be an easy fix there.

Water Marbling with
Nail Polish

Best for the time-poor, great for beginners and fun for the kids – just have some nail polish remover handy.

Many moons ago, when I first fell in love with the art of marbling, I watched a YouTube video of someone marbling with nail polish. I was utterly amazed and – despite it being a terrible video – it inspired me to give it a try. Much of the marbling research I had done had led me to the more time-consuming and costly methods so I found marbling with nail polish to be a really brilliant entry level technique and fairly inexpensive. Nail polish will happily sit on the surface of a water bath and can be used to create a multitude of abstract patterns without needing to manipulate it.

Nail polish dries quickly, so whilst this is an easy technique to start with, it does have its limitations. Work as quickly as you can and don't worry if the polish dries and you need to start again. Just clean the water bath using a strip of scrap paper or newspaper and repeat the process to create more marbled patterns. Different brands of nail polish and different colours will all disperse differently in water so experiment with what you have to hand to see how your colours work. Newer polishes will work best; I'd recommend a non-toxic variety.

Open all bottles of nail polish just before you begin marbling to save time when dropping colour into the water. **Keep windows open so your space is well ventilated when using this technique.**

You will need

Water bath – a shallow tray to fit the object to be marbled comfortably. This will vary from project to project. Nail polish may stain so use a disposable foil tray or an old plastic food packaging tray

Room-temperature distilled water

Scrap paper or newspaper to skim water and clean the excess inks away

3–5 colours of nail polish

Stylus – cocktail sticks (toothpicks) work perfectly here but aren't necessary

Paper or object to marble

1   Fill the water bath two thirds full with distilled water. Let it settle and make sure there are no bubbles on the surface. Use a scrap of newspaper to skim the water to remove any lint or dust that might have fallen in.

2   I'd always recommend starting off with a sample using paper. This way you can test the marbling bath and avoid any disasters before creating your final print. Keep your samples and make notes in your sketchbook as you work.

3 Add the nail polish into the water in random patterns, swirls and dots. Try to pour it as close to the surface as you can to aid in drying time.

4 Work with 2–3 colours to begin with but as your confidence grows play with adding more colours to your bath. Use the brush to splatter the nail polish across the water as well as pouring from the pot.

5 Create an abstract pattern using the pouring technique or use a stylus to manipulate the ink. The nail polish will dry within a few minutes so if you're using a stylus work quickly.

6 Once you are happy with the pattern on the surface of the water, gently bend the paper so it bows into the water at the centre and then gently lower the sides in.

7 You will see the paper saturate with water and inks within a few moments and then it is ready to remove. If using a sturdier card, place it into the water at a 45-degree angle to catch the ink instead. Pick it up on one edge and gently pull away to reveal the print. Shake off any excess water and set aside to dry overnight. Once dry, place under a heavy book or gently iron to flatten and remove any creases caused by the water.

Water Marbling with

Ready-made Pre-mixed Inks

I am a big fan of anything that is going to save time. I often think one of the blocks to trying a new craft is thinking you don't have enough time or that you'll need expensive materials and loads of space to do it in. None of these things is true when it comes to marbling because, thanks to the magic of ready-made inks, the hard work has been done – so I am a big advocate of the pre-mixed marbling ink.

I have tried a range of these types of inks (there are a lot of varieties and brands out there) and my favourite is the Marabu Easy Marble ink because you don't need to make a size or pre-treat the water to allow the inks to float. The base colour palette is vast and you can mix these colours together easily to create an even better range. Like a lot of things in life they might not work out the first time you give them a try, but practice will eventually make perfect. When it comes to marbling, if you don't have a few disasters you're definitely not doing it right.

As with all the water-marbling techniques you'll begin by making your water bath with distilled water, then add droplets of ink into the bath before manipulating and submerging paper or fabric to print.

You will need

Water bath – a shallow tray to fit the object to be marbled comfortably. This will vary from project to project.

Room-temperature distilled water

Scrap paper or newspaper to skim water and clean the excess inks away

3–5 colours of pre-mixed marbling inks

Stylus – cocktail sticks (toothpicks) work perfectly here

Surface or object to marble onto

Keep your space well ventilated when using this technique.

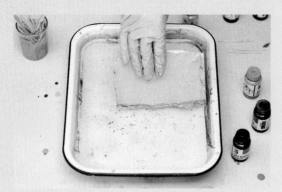

1   Use room-temperature distilled water for best results. Use newspaper or paper strips to skim the water to remove any lint or dust as this can also affect the print.

2   Cover the bath evenly with the first colour, then work into this layer with the remaining colours in your palette. Dropping the ink close to the water will extend its working time.

3   Experiment with the way you drop the inks into the water. Drop by drop works best, but as you grow in confidence feel free to experiment to create more complex patterns.

4   You have around 2 minutes before the inks begin to dry so use a stylus to gently manipulate the ink as speedily as you can to create a variety of unique patterns.

5   Sample all the colours and note down the way each disperses in water. Colours with more pigment will disperse differently to those with a lower pigment, so if you're hoping for a particular effect make sure to sample, sample, sample first. Personally I really enjoy the freedom marbling allows and relish letting myself go and enjoying the organic patterns that can be achieved with this craft.

6   Gently lower your paper, card or object into the water, making sure to catch all of the marbling ink. With paper I recommend either sliding it into the water at a 45-degree angle, bowing it in the centre and then working from the middle out, or lowering it into the water from opposite corner to corner to cover the sheet in pattern.

7   Blow or gently pull away the excess ink on the surface of the water bath before removing the paper or object. The ink will start to turn gloopy as it dries so pull away these strands from your work if any start to appear. Set aside to dry and voilà!

Water Marbling with
Carrageenan Size and Acrylic Paints

This is the most traditional marbling method and one in which you will need to spend a bit more time preparing for the main event. The benefit of this technique is that you will be able to create the most complex patterns without the time limitations of the nail polish and ready-mixed ink methods.

You will also have much more flexibility with your colour palette because it uses acrylic paints, which can be mixed up to create a rainbow of colours to play with. This method will also work with oil paints, gouache and watercolours, as well as on fabric. Although this is one of the more expensive techniques, once mixed the size will usually last for a few days.

You will need

Water bath – shallow tray to fit the object to be marbled comfortably. This will vary from project to project.

Carrageenan

Room temperature distilled water

Measuring scale, jug (pitcher) and spoon

Whisk and blender

Marbling tray

Gloves

Alum

Natural sponge

Fabric, paper or object to marble onto

Pencil

Steam iron

Bowl/bucket to mordant fabric in

Acrylic paints

Jar or pot to mix inks

Eye dropper, pipette or paintbrush

Ox gall or Kodak Photo-Flo

Newspaper scraps to clean excess ink

Drawing board or heavy books (optional)

Preparing the size

The first step in this process is to mix up the size to thicken the water and allow inks to float on the surface. I'm using the lambda grade of carrageenan, which is the best variety for water marbling. Recipes for making this vary due to the nature of the natural Irish moss it is made from and because marbling recipes to this day are still quite secretive. There are many factors that can affect any part of the process of making your size so, as I have said and will keep saying, the key to successful marbling is to practise and make notes as you go. By the time you've had a few goes at making the size you will have your own recipe to follow.

The recipe

1   I'm using 4 teaspoons (19g) of carrageenan to 3.79 litres (1 US gallon) of water.

2   First you will need to blend the carrageenan with around 2 litres (¼ US pints) of warm water. As it is a natural product you can use a kitchen blender (a whisk will work too but will take longer to mix into a smooth paste). Blend thoroughly, you want to dissolve the powder completely to end up with a lump-free smooth liquid.

3   Pour the size into your marbling tray and add the remaining water slowly until you have a wallpaper-paste or honey-like consistency. Whisk gently whilst in the tray to combine the water and smooth out any lumps that might appear.

4   Allow it to rest for at least 6 hours. I've found it works best if you leave it overnight so that the mixture can really settle and any air bubbles will rise to the surface and pop away. Make sure to cover it to avoid any dust or lint falling into the bath.

Mordanting

While you are waiting for your size to be ready you can prepare your paper or fabrics for printing by mordanting them. Mordanting is a way to fix dyes or pigments to surfaces and is often used in the fabric-dyeing process. If you don't prepare your paper or fabrics in this way your beautiful prints will wash right off, which has happened to me on many occasions. It was utterly heartbreaking but was a good lesson to learn, so make sure to take your time preparing your materials.

How to mordant paper:

1   Wear gloves when using alum as it can irritate the skin and make sure you are in a well-ventilated space.

2   Dissolve 2 teaspoons (10g) of alum into a 3.79 litres (1 US gallon) of hot water and stir until the alum has completely dissolved. The recipe varies depending on the manufacturer so do check and follow their guidelines.

3   Use a natural sponge to coat the paper with the alum solution and set aside to dry. You can flatten it out with heavy drawing boards or books. Prepare the papers the day before marbling with them – they will last for a couple of days before the alum starts to oxidise. You could also fill a tray with alum and submerge the paper in the solution if you prefer.

4   Using a pencil, mark the reverse of the paper so you know which side to marble when it comes to it. The alum will dry clear so it's often hard to tell otherwise.

How to mordant fabric

1   Always pre-wash your fabrics to remove any dirt and residue from the manufacturing process. Leave to dry naturally and then gently press.

2   I recommend following the manufacturer's guidelines to create an alum solution for fabric because recipes vary. I usually use a large bowl or bucket and mix a larger quantity, so that I can drop my piece of fabric into it easily.

3   Place the fabric in the bowl or bucket and leave to soak for 20 minutes.

4   Rinse off any excess alum, if recommended in the guidelines. I have found it worked better for me when I didn't rinse the fabric so it's worth trying and testing both methods if you are having trouble with your inks fixing.

5   Then leave to dry naturally and gently press before marbling.

Fixing the paints to fabric

When working with fabric you will need to fix the paint to the fabric by heat setting after 24 hours. To do this, press the fabric using steam and an iron.

As with anything hand-printed, the prints are colour-fast but delicate, so I recommend washing the marbled fabric on a gentle cool cycle or dry cleaning.

Preparing the inks

It's a good idea to prepare your inks in advance to make the marbling process as smooth as can be. Once you have chosen your colour palette (I'd start with 3–5 colours) you'll need to mix the acrylic paint colours.

How to mix your paints:

1   Squeeze a small amount of paint into a pot or jam jar and mix it with water to thin the paint to a milk-like and more inky consistency.

2   This is where a separate sampling marbling bath comes in handy so you can test the paint colours without disrupting the size in the main batch. Using an eye dropper, pipette or brush end, drop/splatter some paint into the size. Make a note of how it spreads because every colour is different and will disperse differently.

3   If the ink sinks, add a drop of dispersant, such as ox gall or Kodak Photo-Flo, to the colour. If it floats, it may not need any dispersant. Repeat the testing process for every colour until you're happy with the way they react in the size.

4   Once you are happy with your colour palette and consistency, mix up more inks depending on the project and quantities you might need.

Ready for marbling

Much like in the previous methods, you will be applying the inks to the water in various patterns and then manipulating the ink in the size. You will quickly notice that the size allows ample time to play with colour and pattern because the inks won't dry in the same way as previous methods. This is the really mesmerising and magical part of the marbling process.

Experimenting with your marbling tools is key to developing your design work, but enjoying the splattering process is just so fun it will evolve naturally. I am a huge fan of the organic patterns and marks that can be made in this process, so make sure to do lots of experimenting! Jot down what works and what doesn't work as you go along, to keep track of your marbling techniques and look back to see how they evolve.

See pages 42–45 for some types of patterns and colour combinations you could work with; there are no rules.

1   When you're happy with the patterns you have created it's time to submerge the paper or fabric into the water. Much as in the previous methods you will dip this into the size at a 45-degree angle or by gently bowing the centre into the water and then lowering the sides. Wait for the ink to coat the surface of the material.

2   You will see the ink saturate the material and at this point remove it, gently scraping off any excess size on the edge of the tray.

3   Gently rinse with clean cold water to remove the size and any ink residue, then set aside to dry. With fabric I tend to swill it around the water to remove the excess size, so as to not remove any paint in the process.

4   Leave to dry naturally. Press flat once dry.

5   Remove any leftover inks from the tray using newspaper strips; they will come away clean when there is no ink left.

6   You can then start again with fresh inks to repeat the process.

The size should last for a few days – even up to a week, depending on the weather. A warm day or a cold day might also affect your size, so keep a note of all these factors and date your work.

I find my size is usually ready to wash away when it becomes too muddy to see the ink colours clearly, or after a good few days of marbling. As the size is a natural product and the paints water-based they can safely be washed in the sink.

Suminagashi Marbling

On my quest to master the art of marbling I was completely mesmerised and drawn to the Japanese suminagashi method. I wanted to share this heritage technique with you all because it dates back to the 12th century and is utterly beautiful. It is also one of the lower maintenance of all the marbling techniques.

Suminagashi means 'floating ink' and it is quite literally that – it comes from the Japanese words *sumi* meaning 'ink' and *nagashi* meaning 'floating'. It uses highly pigmented sumi inks made from burnt pine wood, which are available ready-mixed but also come in a stone form that can be turned into ink using water. It's traditionally a lovely and rich black colour that is brighter and more crisp than Indian ink.

As a print designer I would often look to the works of Japanese artists for inspiration. Their design sensibilities and use of colour were always so intriguing. I collected washi papers and specialist pattern books and was so inspired by the way they worked with colour and illustration, so it felt only natural to explore their awe-inspiring marbling technique. Every single part of the process is beautiful, from the calligraphy sumi brushes to the labels on the inks.

You will need

Water bath – shallow tray to fit the object to be marbled comfortably. This will vary from project to project.

Room-temperature distilled water

Scrap paper or newspaper to skim water and clean the excess inks away

Sumi inks – Japanese-made opaque inks

Jam jars, pots or a palette for mixing inks

Surfactant – Kodak Photo-Flo or washing-up liquid (dish soap)

Sumi brushes – these are used in calligraphy and brush lettering and have a lovely delicate quality

Stylus – a fan, straw or cocktail stick (toothpicks) (get creative!)

Japanese rice paper (optional)

Paper or fabric to print onto

1   Set up the marbling bath; fill your tray with at least 2.5cm (1in) of distilled or soft water. Skim the marbling bath using a strip of newspaper to remove any dust.

2   Ready two coloured inks by pouring a small amount into a jar and diluting with a drop of surfactant. Each ink needs its own brush. Add water, surfactant and a brush to a third jar.

3   Dip the very tip of the brush into the first ink colour – it should have just enough ink to saturate the brush without dripping.

4   Dip the very tip of the brush into the centre of the water. You will see a circle of ink appear. Repeat with colour two, dipping the tip of the brush into the centre again. Repeat with the water and surfactant mix and build a series of concentric circles until the water bath is filled with a pleasing amount of ink.

5   Don't worry if any inks drop to the bottom of the water bath, they won't affect your print. Just add a little more surfactant to help them float.

6   This is such a beautiful technique and a much slower way of marbling. You can manipulate the inks to create patterns in a number of ways:

+ Blowing on the water using your breath or a straw.

+ Gently shuffle the water bath to create patterns in the water.

+ Fan the water to move the inks into a zigzag pattern.

+ Use a stylus as in previous techniques to drag it through the ink to create patterns.

+ Use a stand of your hair! An odd one but a single strand of hair acts as a great tool for pattern making. Some even use cats' whiskers!

7   Print in the same way as the marbling with size technique onto mordanted paper or fabrics (see pages 34 and 37). I like to print onto Japanese rice papers because these are the most traditional materials for the technique. They are wonderfully absorbent and have a beautiful finish.

8   Leave to dry naturally and fix any fabrics using heat after 24 hours. Wash any excess alum from fabrics before using.

9   Use newspaper strips to remove any excess ink on the water and you can then repeat the process again.

As with most Japanese things, sumi brushes will also look beautiful in your workspace. Try to store them flat so they will keep their point.

Patterns

Experimenting with your marbling tools is key to developing your design work. I am a huge fan of the organic patterns and marks that can be made in this process, they are truly mesmerising. Here are a few ideas for you to try.

1 Load your stylus with paint. I find using a wide flat brush works best for the splatter effect. Gently tap the top of the brush over the surface of the water to spray the ink.

2 Vary the size of your drops by raising your pipette higher and lower to alter the pattern.

3 Using a pipette you can drop larger areas of paint into the water.

4 The lighter you tap, the smaller the drops of ink will be – and the firmer you tap, the larger they will be. Experiment and enjoy the process, layering colours to create a pattern.

Swirl / Snail

1 This is one of the easiest and more organic of marbling patterns. Drop the inks into the water bath, using the whole surface with varying levels of vigour!

2 Pull a cocktail stick (toothpick) through the ink and water bath quickly, swirling through the inks as you go to create these stunning patterns.

Gelgit / Chevrons

  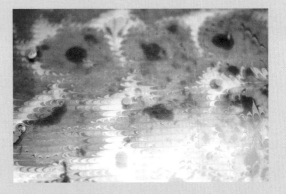

1 The Gelgit or chevron patterns seen in many classic marbling works can be created using the comb tool.

2 Pull the comb through the inks from one end of your water bath to the other. Experiment to create varying chevrons by zigzagging the comb and pulling it back and forth.

Stone

1 This is another classic marbling pattern. Using a pipette or similar dropping tool, create large ink drops within the size bath.

2 Experiment with dropping the ink from varying heights and combine with the swirl and chevron techniques to make even more interesting patterns.

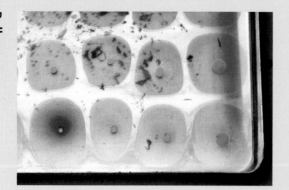

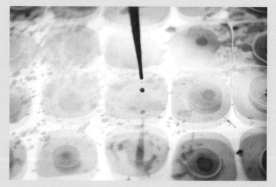

1 Carefully using a pipette, drop one drop of ink into the water bath; it will form a circle.

2 Repeat with a second colour, dropping this into the centre of the circle.

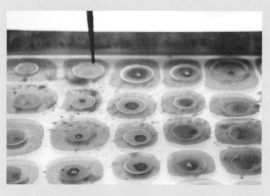

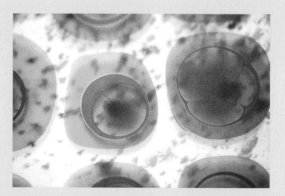

3 Repeat one more time to create the finished bullseye design.

4 Keep going to fill the bath with coloured concentric circles that look like bullseyes.

1 Drop the marbling ink into the water bath to create a larger circle.

2 Use a cocktail stick or similar to pull through the middle of the circle to create a heart shape.

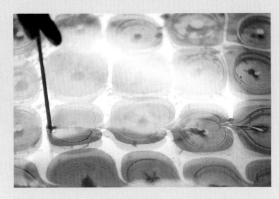

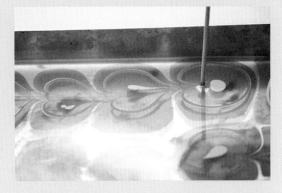

1 Using a stylus (I like to use a cocktail stick here) you can also manipulate the bullseye to create a heart shape.

2 Pull the ink from top to bottom from the middle point of the bullseye.

3 You could also create a flower shape by pulling the ink out evenly from the centre point at similar intervals.

4 Experiment with colours and play with the shapes you can create in water.

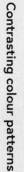

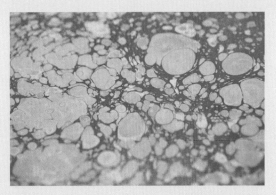

1 Once you are more confident with creating pattern, begin working with contrasting colours to bring your prints to life.

2 Layer colours on top of one another and don't be afraid to really load your brush and marbling bath with inks.

Master the Basics

Now that you're familiar with the techniques, the best way to get to grips with them and really understand the individual processes is to get started. I always recommend beginning your marbling journey with paper. Not only is it the least expensive of materials because you can use papers and cards destined for the recycling bin, it is an excellent way to create a sample library of colours to work with, too.

Paper and card

The world of paper can be quite overwhelming because there are so many varieties, colours and textures to choose from just on the shelves of an art shop – let alone to be found online. When choosing paper for marbling projects first familiarise yourself with the different weights available. I recommend working with paper weights from 80gsm to 350gsm for best results. The latter is a heavier weight and less flexible card stock often used for postcards, and the former a lighter and more flexible paper that's the same weight as the paper you use in a printer. With a heavier weight you won't be able to manipulate the paper as much in the marbling bath – not a bad thing, but lighter weight paper that's easier to manipulate will make life simpler when marbling for the first time. In marbling the inks will be absorbed onto the paper when printed so always opt for an uncoated paper stock, the more absorbent the better. A glossy coated paper won't print and inks will wash right off even with good mordanting.

When working with paper and card during your marbling journey, set aside time at the start to cut larger sheets down to fit comfortably inside your marbling bath. Around 1–2cm (⅜–¾in) smaller than the size of the tray works perfectly. This will ensure the print covers the entire surface of the paper.

Notecards and envelopes

As a huge stationery fiend I began my marbling journey with paper and often made notecards, greetings cards, tags and matching envelopes as gifts and to send to friends and family. It's a lovely way to give a second life to envelopes and notecards destined for the waste bin. Marbling over the top of old Christmas or birthday cards is another nice way to give them a second life. I often use a paper punch to create shapes that can then be collaged to create art for my walls, or more cards or even stitched into garlands.

Card coasters

I love marbling everyday objects and things that have a purpose or bring joy to simple tasks, like making a cup of tea. Meet the humble card coaster. I started marbling ceramic coasters, but before I felt confident enough to have a go on ceramics I wanted to try my marbling skills on something less precious. I found these card coasters/beer mats and now they've become a staple in my marbling cabinet. I like to give a matching set as a gift with a bottle of something sparkling for special occasions.

The art of marbling is more than just a craft — it is such a versatile technique and can be applied to absolutely anything. All you need to do is use your creativity. In this chapter you'll find some of my favourite projects, from nail art to silk fabric scrap scrunchies.

lifestyle

Ruffled Headband

You might have noticed I am a big fan of a hair accessory. Here's a great way to use up leftover fabrics by creating a beautiful ruffled headband. It's a super simple sewing project, too, so a fabulous way to start off your sewing journey.

You will need

Marbling with fabric materials and tools as listed on page 33

Fabric – silk or cotton, 3–4 times the length of your headband by twice the width plus a 1.5cm (⅝in) seam allowance

Measuring tape

Scissors

Iron and ironing board

Pins

Invisible marker or a pencil

Sewing machine and matching thread

Loop turner or safety pin

Plain headband

Glue gun and glue sticks

10cm (4in) of grosgrain ribbon (optional)

Technique

We'll be using marbling with size to marble fabric in the first part of this project. Refer to pages 33–39 for the full method and best practices, page 140 for troubleshooting and the Scrunchie project on page 60.

Preparation

When working with fabric marbling, always pre-wash your fabrics to avoid any shrinkage later down the line and to remove any residue that may still be on the fabric from the manufacturing process. Leave the fabric to dry naturally.

You will need to prepare a marbling bath with size and mordant your fabrics in advance of this project.

How to

Measure and cut out your pre-washed and mordanted fabric pieces, ready to marble them.

Print your fabric pieces using the marbling with size technique, rinse and leave to dry naturally.

Press the fabric and fold right sides together, pinning along the long edge at right angles – as in the scrunchie project you will sew a channel.

Before you sew the channel, taper the ends. Measure around 2.5cm (1in) from the edge of the fabric and mark. Then measure the width of the headband and mark on the opening of the channel.

Draw a line to join the two marks at each end; this will taper the bottom of the headband to fold neatly into place.

Stitch with a sewing machine and matching thread from one end of the headband to the other.

Remove the pins and turn the fabric right side out. Use a loop turner if you have one, or a safety pin will work, too – pin to one end and feed it through the channel.

Press with the seam in the centre.

Feed the headband through the channel, gathering the fabric evenly and placing the seam on the underside.

Using the glue gun, glue one end into place at a time. The headband is ready to wear as soon as the glue is dry.

If you wish, bind each end of the headband with grosgrain ribbon for a professional touch.

Socks

One of the best ways you can bring some mood-boosting colour therapy into your everyday life is with the addition of a colourful sock. Especially if, like my husband, you have a pile of what were once white and are now grey socks that need some love. By marbling them you'll give them the refresh they need and spread the bug for dopamine dressing. They also make excellent and inexpensive gifts for friends as you really can't have too many pairs of socks in my opinion!

You will need

Marbling with fabric materials
and tools as listed on page 33

Wide card to slip inside the socks
to stretch them when printing

Cotton socks

Iron and ironing board

Technique

We'll be using marbling with size to marble fabric in the
first part of this project. Refer to pages 33–39 for the full
method and page 140 for troubleshooting.

Preparation

When working with fabric marbling, always pre-wash your
fabrics to avoid any shrinkage later down the line and to
remove any residue that may still be on the fabric from the
manufacturing process. Leave the fabric to dry naturally.

You will need to prepare a marbling bath with size and
mordant your fabrics in advance of this project.

How to

Following the instructions for marbling with size to
prepare the bath.

Place a piece of wide card inside each sock. This is to
stretch the fabric out as it would be when worn, so the
print shows clearly.

Print one side at a time, being mindful of where the print
will join on the socks.

Remove the socks from the size. Scrape any excess size
off on the edge of the tray and gently rinse/swill any size
away in water.

Leave to dry naturally and then press to heat-fix the socks.

Wash on a cool wash cycle to remove any alum before
wearing the socks.

Scrunchie

One of my favourite simple sewing projects is to make a scrunchie; not only is it a great way to use up any fabric scraps you have hanging around but it also makes a wonderful 90s-vibe hair accessory or the perfect gift for your BFF. I'm a big fan of natural fabrics and texture so I usually make my scrunchies using linen, cotton or silk fabric scraps. Silk scrunchies are also much better for tying your hair back because they reduce hair breakage so definitely worth sewing a few of these, too. Once you make one you won't be able to stop, I guarantee it.

You will need

Marbling with fabric materials and tools as listed on page 33

Fabric – 57 x 11cm (22½ x 4½in) including a 1.5cm (⅝in) seam allowance

Iron and ironing board

Fabric scissors

Tape measure

Pins

Sewing machine and matching thread (optional)

Elastic – approx. 30cm (12in) by 6mm (¼in) wide

Safety pin

Hand sewing needle and matching thread

> I always cut my fabric pieces out before marbling to avoid creating fabric waste – and I can also create a more planned marbled pattern for the exact area of fabric that will be seen in the project.

Technique

We'll be using marbling with size to marble fabric in the first part of this project which will then be sewn into your scrunchie. Refer to pages 33–39 for the full method and page 140 for troubleshooting.

Preparation

When working with fabric marbling, always pre-wash your fabrics to avoid any shrinkage later down the line and to remove any residue that may still be on the fabric from the manufacturing process. Leave the fabric to dry naturally.

You will need to prepare a marbling bath with size and mordant your fabrics in advance of this project.

How to

Press, measure and cut out your fabric pieces. Once the fabric is mordanted and dry, press once more so it is crease-free and ready to marble.

Using the marbling with size technique, create patterns in the marbling bath using the acrylic paints. I recommend doing test samples on smaller squares of fabric to perfect the paint density because it can often appear paler on fabric than paper so you may want to add more paint to the bath.

Once you are happy with your patterns in the marbling bath, carefully marble the fabric. If the fabric is larger than the tray to hand you can marble sections at a time, but place the marbled sections into water while you do the next section. I love the organic effect this creates with the marbled patterns on fabric.

When the fabric is completely marbled, scrape the size on the edge of the tray, then rinse off any excess size by gently swilling it in water. Avoid any force here so as not to remove the paint. Hang to dry naturally. Silk usually dries very quickly and can be sewn straight away.

Continued on next page

Sewing the scrunchie

Press the fabric once more to remove any creases from the marbling.

Fold the fabric in half right sides together down the length. Pin at right angles along the long edge at 1.5cm (⅝in) intervals to hold the fabric in place.

Set up your sewing machine with matching thread and stitch with a 1.5cm (⅝in) seam allowance along the long side of the fabric. Leave a gap of about 2cm (¾in) at the start and end of the seam. You could hand sew this seam if you don't have a sewing machine.

You have now sewn a channel. Turn the fabric right side out and press once more.

Measure and cut a length of elastic to size. I usually measure this by wrapping the elastic around my wrist and then adding about 2.5cm (1in) extra at either end to allow for knotting the ends.

Attach a safety pin to one end of the elastic. Whilst holding onto the other end, feed the safety pin through the fabric channel until both ends meet. Tie the ends of the elastic together with a strong knot.

Turn the raw edges of the fabric inside at either end and press into place, then tuck one end inside the other. Pin into place and finish by hand sewing the edges together for a neat and invisible finish using an invisible whip stitch. You can also sew across the seam using your machine – this will leave a visible sewing line that is less tidy but once the scrunchie is on it isn't noticeable.

Zhoosh the ruffles into place by spreading the fabric out evenly around the elastic and tada! Your scrunchie is ready to wear!

Other ideas

+ You can easily vary the measurements to create wider or thinner scrunchies. Try 5cm (2in) wide for a skinny scrunchie or 22cm (8½in) for a wider one.

+ If you're a confident sewist you could add a matching ribbon to the middle or a lace trim in between the seam.

If you can't fit the full length of fabric into the marbling bath, cut smaller pieces that can be sewn together later to create a longer length.

Ruffled Collar

One of the first things I taught myself how to sew was a simple Peter Pan collar, tracing a pattern from a vintage shirt – I was so pleased with it. My teenage self would be super-proud her sewing skills have evolved since then and I'm excited to share this ruffle collar with you. I love accessorising these over plain T-shirts, sweatshirts and knits to bring a little fun and colour to an outfit in an instant.

You will need

Marbling with fabric materials and tools as listed on page 33

Template or existing collar to copy

Paper for pattern

Pencil

Paper scissors

Fabric – approx. 40 x 40cm (16 x 16in), I used 100% cotton

Pins

Invisible marker (optional)

Fabric scissors

Sewing machine and matching thread

Velvet ribbon – 2 lengths, each 10mm (⅜in) wide x 46cm (18in)

Hand sewing needle and matching thread

Iron and ironing board

Technique

We'll be using marbling with size to marble fabric in the first part of this project. Refer to pages 33–39 for the full method and page 140 for troubleshooting.

Preparation

When working with fabric marbling, always pre-wash your fabrics to avoid any shrinkage later down the line and to remove any residue that may still be on the fabric from the manufacturing process. Leave the fabric to dry naturally.

You will need to prepare a marbling bath with size and mordant your fabrics in advance of this project.

How to

Trace an existing shirt collar onto paper to make a pattern, adding a 1.5cm (⅝in) seam allowance, or trace the template on page 70.

Cut out the pattern and check it fits around your neck. Adjust it if necessary – test the paper pattern first before cutting out your fabric.

Fold the fabric in half and lay the pattern onto it with the fold line aligned with the fabric fold. Pin in place – or draw around the template using an invisible marker if it is easier. Cut the shape out using fabric scissors, being careful to avoid the pins. Repeat so you have two fabric pieces, one for the front and one for the reverse of the collar.

Print your fabric pieces using the marbling with size technique, rinse and leave to dry naturally.

For the ruffle cut a 4 x 50cm (1½ x 20in) length of fabric. Press in half wrong sides together, tucking the raw ends inside for a neat ruffle end. Set your sewing machine to the longest straight stitch and sew two rows of gathering stitches down the long edge, leaving the ends of the threads loose.

Pull the threads on each end to gather the fabric, evenly spreading the fabric ruffles down the length. This step does take a while so don't rush it.

Continued on next page

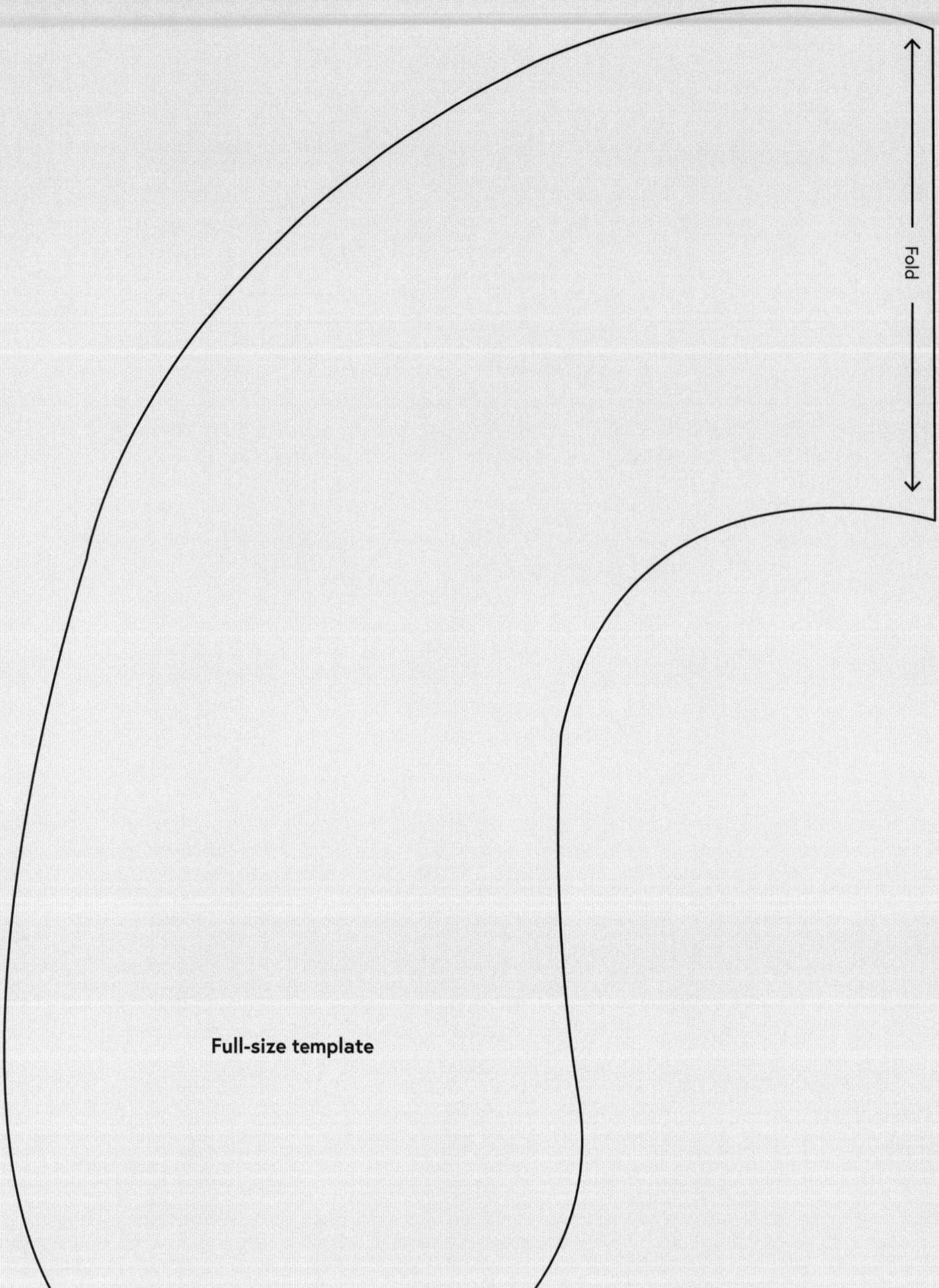

Fold

Full-size template

With the right side of the front collar facing up, place the ribbon neck ties on top with one end of each 1.5cm (⅝in) down from the top edge. The ribbons should lie over the collar piece right sides together, with one end aligned with the raw edge on either side. Pin the ribbon ends in place.

Pin the ruffle onto the collar all around the bottom edge, with raw edges aligned and starting from the neck tie. Make sure the ruffles are evenly spread all around.

Stitch the ruffle in place using a 1.5cm (⅝in) seam allowance. Remove the pins.

Lay the collar back piece on top, with ruffle and neck ties sandwiched between the two collar layers. Pin in place.

Sew around through all layers with a 1.5cm (⅝in) seam allowance. Leave a gap of 10cm (4in) at the inside back edge so you can turn the collar right side out.

Cut notches into the curves and trim the ends, then turn the collar right side out.

Press, turn the edges of the gap inside the collar, then press and hand stitch closed with an invisible whip stitch.

Use a contrasting colour fabric for the reverse of the collar and make it double-sided. Contrast colour fabrics also work beautifully for the ruffle.

You can adjust the fabric length for the ruffle depending on how gathered you'd like the ruffle to be or you can remove the ruffle entirely.

Phone Case

You will need

Rubbing alcohol

Lint-free cloth

Shallow dish or tray

Room-temperature distilled water

Marabu Easy Marble inks suitable
for all surfaces

Gloves

Stylus

Phone case – clear plastic or
a pale colour will work best, they
are readily available online

Drying space

Spray clear matt varnish

One of the things I love most about marbling is that you can apply the technique to pretty much anything. I was running a marbling workshop last year and one of my students was so excited about the technique that she had quickly run out of things to marble – so she pulled her phone case from her phone to marble it too. It is such a lovely way to personalise and add some colour to such an everyday item.

Technique

We'll be using water marbling with ready-made inks for this project. Refer to pages 30–32 for the full method and page 140 for troubleshooting.

Preparation

Clean your phone case with a lint-free cloth and a little rubbing alcohol to remove and dust or oils from your hands that may prevent the inks from sticking when marbling.

How to

First fill your tray two-thirds full with room-temperature water.

Drop the first ink colour into the tray, making sure to cover the surface of the water.

Next drop any other colours into the water. You can manipulate the colours to create your design but remember to work quickly because the inks will dry after a couple of minutes.

When you are happy with the design and placement of the inks in the water bath, dip your phone case into the bowl to submerge the area you'd like the ink to cover. Try to place the case into the water at a slight angle, this will help avoid any air bubbles and ensure full coverage.

Blow or push away any excess ink from the case and remove from the tray to reveal your printed phone case!

Leave to dry for at least 24 hours, and then spray with varnish to protect the delicate pattern. Once dry it's ready to use.

Nail Art

Marbling isn't just for paper, card or fabric: it can be recreated on your nails, too. Nail art is incredibly therapeutic and I find it a really brilliant way to escape my screen and create a daily joy – it is all about the little things in life and catching a glimpse of some beautifully marbled nails is a real joy bringer. No need for expensive or professional tools either, here's how to marble yours…

You will need

Nail polish remover

Cotton pads

Cuticle pusher (optional)

Buffer (optional)

Base coat

Small shallow tray

Distilled water

2–3 colours of nail polish

Stylus (optional)

Washi tape (optional)

Top coat

Flat dish or surface for nail polish (optional)

Technique

We'll be using water marbling with nail polish for this project. Refer to pages 28–29 for the full method and page 140 for troubleshooting.

Preparation

Remove any existing nail polish from your nails with nail polish remover. If you are confident in cleaning your cuticles go ahead and do this now with a cuticle pusher or cuticle remover, then gently buff the surface of the nail to remove any natural oils from the surface of the nail bed.

I like to give my nails a clear or pale coloured base coat of polish as it creates a nicer finish for the marbled effect which will sit on top of this layer.

How to

Create your marbling bath. Once you are happy with the patterns in the bath, one at a time dip your nails into the water to create a marbled nail effect.

Either wipe away any excess nail polish from your finger using nail polish remover and a cotton pad or mask your finger with washi tape or similar before dipping.

Leave to dry before repeating the process for the next nail. Finish with a top coat to seal and protect the design.

Because this is a time-consuming technique I tend to choose one or two nails to feature a marbled pattern. If you have all the time in the world then definitely go all out and marble all of your nails.

The lazy way: a little hack to create a similar marbled effect is to use a dish to drop 3 to 4 different coloured blobs of nail polish into. Dollop them next to each other and then, with the last coloured brush, scoop all the paint up onto the brush and gently brush across the nail bed to 'marble' the colours together. The effect is easily achieved without too much manipulation and it is really fun and much quicker!

Experiment with your colour palette, perhaps each nail could have a different colour combo!

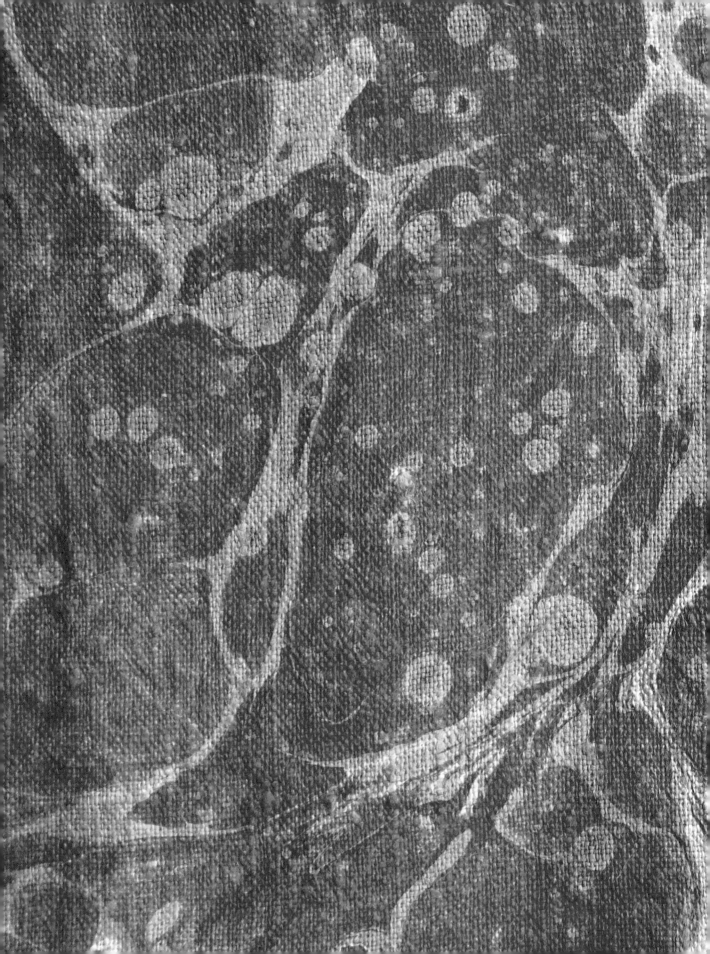

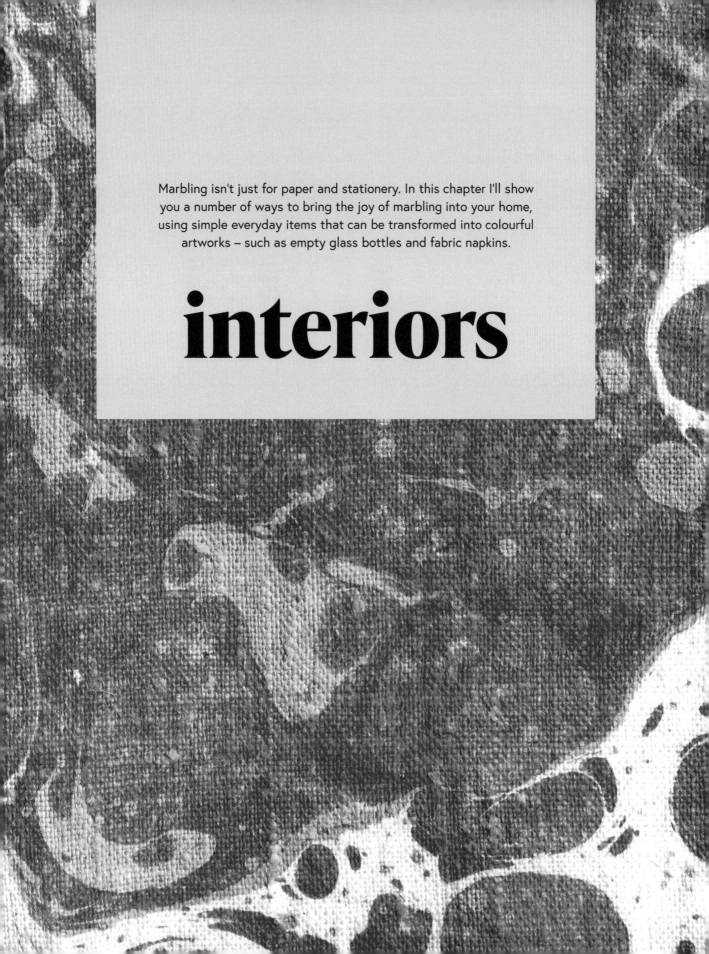

Marbling isn't just for paper and stationery. In this chapter I'll show you a number of ways to bring the joy of marbling into your home, using simple everyday items that can be transformed into colourful artworks – such as empty glass bottles and fabric napkins.

interiors

Candles

These pretty marbled candles are the perfect addition to any tablescape. I love laying the table and inviting friends and family over on the spur of the moment and I always keep a stash of candles in the cupboard to zhoosh up my table. One of my first jobs was as a waitress for black-tie events to which I owe all my table setting know-how and wine glass appreciation. I always start with a colour theme for my tablescape, matching candles and other accessories to my tablecloth and napkins. If you want to jazz up a wooden table or simple tablecloth too, then this is a great way to add some colour and creativity to your table.

You will need

Rubbing alcohol

Lint-free cloth

Taper or dinner candles

Marbling tray – long enough to fit
the candles, a bowl will also work
if you plan on dipping just one end
of the candles

Room-temperature distilled water

Enamel paints in 2–3 colours – you
could use more for a more varied
effect, but when marbling coloured
candles consider how the colours
work together and maybe reduce the
palette to just two colours, with the
third being your candles

Candle holders to place wet candles
in to dry upright

Technique

We'll be using water marbling with ready-made inks for this
project. Refer to pages 30–32 for the full method and page
140 for troubleshooting.

Preparation

Using the cloth and a small amount of rubbing alcohol,
wipe the candles free of any dust and surface residue.
This will give you a clean surface to marble onto.

How to

Fill the tray with about 2.5cm (1in) of water, or if using
a bowl fill it two thirds of the way up with water.

Enamel paints, like nail polish, will dry very quickly so I'd
recommend pouring them into your water bath in spirals
or circles and creating patterns that will transfer onto your
candles without any manipulation. You can test the colours
out in a smaller water bath first to see how they disperse;
as with all paints the varying pigments will work differently.

When happy with your design, dip your candles into the
water and pull out to reveal the pattern!

Leave to dry upright in a candle holder for a few hours
before they are ready to use.

Use non-toxic paints
for safety and avoid
solvent-based
flammable paints
because the candles
will be lit.

Shake and open
all the paints
before you get
started to ensure
no delays during
the process.

Pour the paints
as close to the
water as you can to
aid with the fast
drying time.

Lampshade

Once you've got the hang of marbling you'll want
to marble everything in sight and when I spotted
a plain lampshade at home I knew instantly it needed
a boost of colour and pattern. This is an inexpensive
way to zhoosh up your bedroom lamps – and marbled
lampshades create a luxurious and chic feel and can
really elevate a space. You could even make a matching
cushion or bolster to finish it off. The important thing
to remember is that this technique isn't limited to just
paper and card or the size of the marbling bath. It
can be applied to everything and anything and can
be incredibly transformational.

You will need

Marbling with fabric materials and tools as listed on page 33

Plain fabric lampshade

Damp cloth

Large bucket, tray or bowl that the lampshade will fit inside

Steam iron

Technique

We'll be using marbling with size to marble fabric in this project. Refer to pages 33–39 for the full method and page 140 for troubleshooting.

Preparation

As lampshades are difficult to pre-wash, gently wipe any dust or dirt away with a damp cloth. Leave the fabric to dry naturally.

You will need to prepare a marbling bath with size and mordant your lampshade in advance of this project.

How to

Follow the instructions for marbling with size and dip the lampshade or roll it across the water bath.

Depending on the size of your water bath and lampshade, you can choose to dip a section of the lampshade or marble a larger surface area.

After printing the lampshade, rinse away any excess size with clean water.

Leave to dry naturally and heat-fix gently with steam.

Ruffled Patchwork Cushion

Patchwork is having a huge moment on the catwalks and in sustainable fashion circles and I am a huge fan. It's a great way to save offcuts, samples and scraps from ending up in landfill. They can be used to sew any number of items – here I'll show you how to create this very simple and beautiful cushion using patchworking. It's the perfect project for any of your fabric samples that turned out well, too.

You will need

Marbling with fabric materials and tools as listed on page 33

Fabric squares – I used a lightly textured 100% linen which I love for interiors projects. For a 35cm (14in) square cushion cover, cut each square to 20.5 x 20.5cm (8 x 8in)

Measuring tape

Fabric scissors

Pins

Sewing machine and matching thread

Iron and ironing board

Backing fabric – 20.5 x 20.5cm (8 x 8in)

Knitting needle or similar (optional)

Hand sewing needle and matching thread

Cushion pad 40 x 40cm (16 x 16in)

For the backing fabric I like to use a contrasting colour, or patterned cotton, linen or velvet.

Technique

We'll be using marbling with size to marble fabric in the first part of this project. Refer to pages 33–39 for the full method and page 140 for troubleshooting.

Preparation

When working with fabric marbling, always pre-wash your fabrics to avoid any shrinkage later down the line and to remove any residue that may still be on the fabric from the manufacturing process. Leave the fabric to dry naturally.

You will need to prepare a marbling bath with size and mordant your fabrics in advance of this project.

How to

Measure and cut out your pre-washed fabric squares, and mordant ready to marble them.

Print your fabric squares using the marbling with size technique, rinse and leave to dry naturally.

Lay all four fabric squares out onto a surface and arrange so they feel visually pleasing. Make note or take a photo of the order of these.

Take the top two squares and fold the left square over the right with right sides together. Pin (at right angles) along the left-hand side at 1cm (⅜in) intervals or thereabouts Sew with a 1.5cm (⅝in) seam allowance along the left-hand edge and press the seam open.

Repeat the previous step with the bottom two fabric squares.

You now have two fabric rectangles ready to stitch together. Fold the top rectangle down on top of the bottom one with right sides together.

Carefully pin together making sure the centre points join perfectly because this is the centre of the patchwork cushion. I often tack (baste) the centre into place so it doesn't move on the sewing machine to get a perfect join.

Sew with a 1.5cm (⅝in) seam allowance. Remove the pins and press the seam open. Trim away any excess seam allowance.

Continued on next page

Note: If you would like to add a ruffle to your cushion see the instructions on the right and add at this stage of the project. It is optional but really elevates this simple cushion shape.

Place the fabric for the cushion back right sides together on top of the marbled fabric patchwork. Pin together at right angles around the entire cushion leaving a 15cm (6in) gap in the centre of one edge.

Stitch around the cushion with a 1.5cm (⅝in) seam allowance, leaving the gap unsewn and reversing at the start and finish.

Trim any excess seam allowance and turn the cover right side out, pulling the fabric through the gap in the stitching.

Press once more and turn the edges of the gap inside the cushion. You can use a knitting needle or similar to ease the corners of the cushion out neatly.

Fill with the cushion pad and sew the gap closed using an invisible whip stitch.

Note: If you're a confident sewist why not add an invisible zip to the bottom of your cushion to allow removal of the cushion pad.

Fabric care

Sponge clean or dry clean. If you added a zip you can remove the cover and place on a cool wash cycle.

How to sew a ruffle

You will need a large length of fabric 15 x 350cm (6 x 138in) to create your ruffle. You can sew multiple smaller pieces together to create this longer length. The joins won't be seen once the ruffle is gathered.

With right sides together, join the ends of the strip to form a loop. Fold the strip in half down the length with wrong sides together and press.

On the longest stitch setting, sew two rows of gathering stitches along the raw edge.

Gather the fabric until it measures the same length as around the outside edge of your cushion cover.

With right sides together sandwich the ruffle between the two cushion pieces with raw edges aligned. Pin the three layers of fabric together.

Stitch around the entire cushion with a 1.5cm (⅝in) seam allowance. Use a heavier duty needle if you're working with heavyweight fabric. Leave a 15cm (6in) gap to slip the cushion pad inside or leave your zip open a small way so the cushion can be turned right side out.

Remove the pins and trim any excess fabric.

Turn the cushion right side out, pop in the cushion pad and either hand stitch the gap closed or sew very close to the edge on a sewing machine for a quick finish. If you added a zip, pull the cushion through the zip and add the cushion pad.

Use an unpicker to remove any exposed gathering stitches. Press with an iron and tada! Your cushion is complete!

Vase

You will need

Deep bowl or bucket with enough room to submerge the vessel to be marbled fully

Room-temperature distilled water

Marbling inks suitable for glass in 2–3 colours – I used Marabu Easy Marble solvent-based inks

Gloves

Cocktail sticks or wooden skewers

Clear glass jam jars or bottles

Drying space

Spray clear varnish

Try dipping the vessel into the inks at a 45-degree angle to create some variety to your patterns. Jars can be decorated and used as tea light holders.

This is one of my favourite marbling makes as it's such a quick and easy creative transformation project. It's waste friendly too and is a brilliant upcycling project – take an empty jam jar or glass soda bottle and turn it into a colourful and chic statement vase in a matter of minutes. This is also one of my go-to gifts because they are such lovely presents; gift them with some added dried or fresh flowers and a ribbon tie to make it extra special.

Technique

We'll be using water marbling with ready-made inks for this project. Refer to pages 30–32 for the full method and page 140 for troubleshooting.

Preparation

Clean the glass vessel thoroughly using soap and water, then rinse carefully as any soapy residue will affect your marbling inks.

How to

Fill the bucket or bowl two thirds full with water.

Drop inks into the water bath as per the technique.

Dip the vessel into the water bath, then pull away to reveal the pattern.

The vessel will be touch dry after 20 minutes but I'd leave the glass to dry completely for 24 hours.

Seal the marbling print with some spray varnish for a nice even finish and to protect it from any wear and tear.

Picture Frame

You will need

Fine sandpaper

Wood picture frame with mount

Damp lint-free cloth

Paint sample pot and paintbrush

Marbling tray that the picture frame and mount will fit inside

Room-temperature distilled water

Marbling inks suitable for all surfaces

Gloves

Stylus

Spray clear matt varnish

You could use contrasting colours for the frame and mount to make it pop or try similar tones or varying the pattern scale – have fun!

This is a really fun way to bring some colour into your home and give some life to a plain picture frame. Framing collected ephemera adds so much personality to a space: photo-booth snaps or Polaroids, pressed flowers or stamps, a little sketch – all will look beautiful in a marbled frame.

Technique

We'll be using water marbling using ready-made inks for this project. Refer to pages 30–32 for the full method and page 140 for troubleshooting.

Preparation

Lightly sand the picture frame, wipe with a damp cloth to remove dust and paint. I'd suggest two coats and sufficient drying time before the frame is ready to marble. You could paint the mount to match as we'll be marbling this also.

How to

Fill the tray two thirds full with water. Drop the first ink colour into the tray to cover the surface of the water.

Next drop any other colours in. You can manipulate the colours to create your design but work quickly as the inks will dry after a couple of minutes.

When you are happy with the design and placement of the inks in the bath, submerge the frame into the tray to marble it.

Blow or push away any excess ink from the surface of the water and remove the frame from the tray. Set aside to dry.

Clean away leftover ink in the tray using a scrap of paper or newspaper, then repeat the process to marble the mount.

Leave to dry for at least 24 hours, then spray with matt varnish to protect the pattern. Once dry it's ready to use.

Wall Art

A little something for the interior lover! It's a fact that I am an interiors addict and believe the same rules that you might apply to your wardrobe and the way you get dressed every day can be applied to the way you think about the design and decor within your home.

A great way to add some colour, personality and interest to your home is by creating a gallery wall. Not only is it an impactful way to add some creativity and interest to a boring white wall, it can also be an inexpensive way to jazz up a rented property, too. If you can't use nails try command strips; they are a great removable way to 'hang' your art. Gallery wall, here you come!

A gallery wall need not cost the earth – I love collecting postcards, stamps and packaging that inspire me and always keep them to put into frames for my gallery wall. Until I am able to invest in some posh art, I am much more in favour of creating my own, and a marbled piece of art is a brilliant way to make something truly unique and inject some colour into your living space.

Gesso is a brilliant hand-made surface for marbling onto – it's a very smooth wooden board that has been primed with an acrylic-like paint to create a hard surface.

You will need

A tray large enough to fit your gesso board with space around the edge. It should be deep enough to submerge the board fully

---

Room-temperature distilled water

Marbling inks suitable for ceramic and glass – I used Marabu Easy Marble solvent-based inks

---

Gloves

Cocktail sticks

Gesso board

Drying space

Spray clear varnish

Technique

We'll be using water marbling using ready-made inks for this project. Refer to pages 30–32 for the full method and page 140 for troubleshooting.

Preparation

Choose the ink colours you'd like to use for the project and the type of pattern. As this is a larger project I'd recommend sampling your design on A4 paper or card to make sure the colour combinations and patterns are what you're expecting. There's nothing worse than rushing a project and not getting the results you were hoping for.

Marbling is an art and like all art forms requires practice and patience.

How to

Once you're happy with your design and palette, drop the inks into the water. Make sure to cover the water with one colour fully and then add the other colours.

You might notice some colours disperse more than others and that's down to the pigments. I like to keep notes on the ink colours to better inform my designs.

Submerge the gesso board into the water so it catches the pigment and transfers through the water. Lift to remove the board and reveal the pattern.

Leave to dry overnight. Varnish to protect the surface from wear and tear before hanging it up.

I like to create these in threes. Odd numbers are more pleasing to the eye and a set of three on your wall will always look lovely together.

Plant Pot

I live in a little rented flat in Hackney with my husband, and when we first moved in we were both keen to introduce as much colour into our home as we could (the walls were very brilliant white!). A great way to add colour to stark white walls is to bring some greenery indoors. Green is one of the most calming colours and one of the reasons we find being in nature so relaxing, so stock up on your succulents and bring the garden inside. I often propagate plants and love giving them as gifts in hand-marbled pots. This is a great way to give a concrete or ceramic pot some colour and create a unique treasure for your home or a loved one. It's also a really thoughtful gift and won't break the bank.

You will need

Rubbing alcohol

Lint-free cloth

Concrete or ceramic pot – glass jars or empty candle pots will also work really well

Deep bowl or bucket

Room-temperature distilled water

Marabu Easy Marble inks suitable for all surfaces – or nail polish will work equally well on this surface

Stylus

Gloves

Spray clear varnish

Drying space

Technique

We'll be using water marbling with ready-made inks for this project. Refer to pages 30–32 for the full method and page 140 for troubleshooting.

Preparation

Use rubbing alcohol and a lint free cloth to give the pots a good clean, removing any residue or dirt as this can affect the marbling process.

How to

First fill your bowl or bucket two thirds full with room-temperature water. Drop the first ink colour into the bowl or bucket, making sure to cover the surface of the water.

Next drop any other colours into the water. You can manipulate the colours to create your design, but remember to work quickly because the inks will dry after a couple of minutes.

When you are happy with the design and placement of the inks in the bath, dip your plant pot into the bowl to submerge the area you'd like the ink to cover.

Blow or push away any excess ink from the surface of the water and remove the pot from the bowl to reveal your printed design.

Leave to dry for at least 24 hours. Spray with varnish to protect the delicate pattern. Once dry it's ready to use.

Candle Holder

If you're a huge lover of a tablescape like me, these marbled candle holders will add that attention to detail to your dinner plans. You can pick up clear glass or wooden candle holders second hand or in your local charity shop and give them a second life. I love adding some bright colour to mine to lift a simple dinner table; they bring instant joy.

Harriet

Harriet

You will need

Fine sandpaper

Lint-free cloth

Wooden candle holder

Paint sample pot and paintbrush

Tray or bowl large enough to hold the candle holder

Room-temperature distilled water

Marbling inks suitable for wood

Stylus

Gloves

Drying space

Technique

We'll be using water marbling with ready-made inks for this project. Refer to pages 30–32 for the full method and page 140 for troubleshooting.

Preparation

Gently send the candle holder with fine sandpaper if it has a coating. Clean using a lint-free cloth to make sure it is dust free ready for painting.

Paint the candle stick holder – I'd recommend two lighter coats of matt paint, leaving to dry between coats and for at least 24 hours before it is ready to marble.

How to

Fill your tray or bowl two thirds full with water. Drop the first ink colour into the tray, making sure to cover the surface of the water.

Next drop any other colours into the water. You can manipulate the colours to create your design, but remember to work quickly as the inks will dry after a couple of minutes.

When you are happy with the design and placement of the inks in the bath, roll the candle holder across the surface of the water to ensure it is coated with ink. Alternatively you could use a deep bowl or cover just one end of the holder.

Blow or push away any excess ink from the surface of the water and remove the candle holder from the tray to reveal it in its printed glory! Set aside to dry.

Head to the place settings on page 134 and napkins on page 130 to complete the table.

You could use this technique to marble a collection of candle holders of varying materials. Glass and enamel candle holders would look lovely styled together.

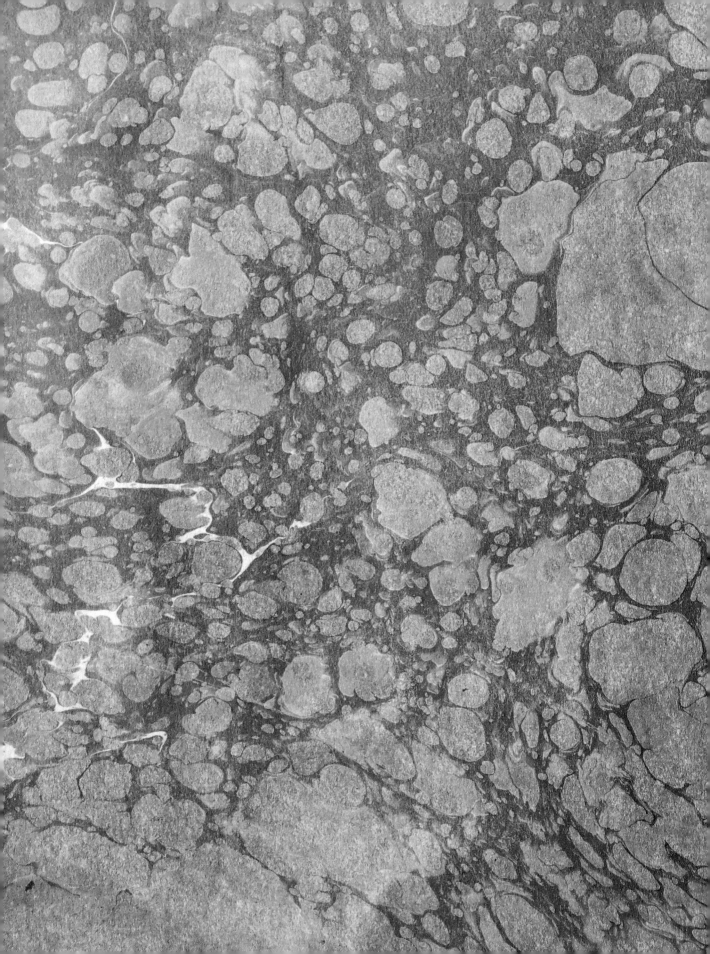

As someone who loves decorating my home for an occasion, here are some fabulous and fun ways to adorn your living space. Whether it's napkins for a dinner party with friends, gift wrap galore for all the birthday gifts you need to wrap or baubles for the Christmas tree, I've got you covered.

seasonal

Gift Wrap

Up your gift wrapping game with a matchy matchy marbled collection of wraps, tags and ribbons. The nature of marbling and the unique patterns it creates give this technique such a luxurious and high-end feel. You'll often see it in luxury packaging so here's how you can create your own. I always like to go the extra mile with gift wrapping because I find it such a joyful experience making my own papers, wrapping gifts and giving them to loved ones – so here are some ways to add that extra level of detail to your gift wrapping.

Other ideas

+ Why not create a more sustainable version of this gift wrap and create a Japanese *furoshiki* wrapping cloth. A 40 x 40cm (16 x 16in) piece of cotton or silk will make a gorgeous wrapping for a small gift. See pages 33–39 for how to marble onto fabric.

+ I like to save ribbons I am gifted over the years and always reuse them for crafting and gifting. Try marbling them to give them a new lease of life and burst of colour. See pages 33–39 for how to marble onto fabric.

+ Invest in a large paper and card punch to create your own gift tags from card and paper scraps. These come in a variety of shapes and sizes and I love reusing paper packaging for marbling, then punching out shapes. You could also create a simple decorative garland by stitching through the shapes on a sewing machine, or use the shapes for collage.

You will need

Large tray that your paper size will fit in comfortably

Room-temperature distilled water

Marbling inks suitable for paper

Stylus

Gloves

Paper (A3 size will wrap a small gift) – see the paper and card section on page 48 for guidance on what types of paper will work best

Drying space

Heavy board or books

Technique

We'll be using water marbling with ready-made inks for this project. Refer to pages 30–32 for the full method and page 140 for troubleshooting.

Preparation

If you're planning on marbling fabric and ribbon, follow the method to prepare your materials for marbling as detailed on pages 33–39.

How to

Fill your tray two thirds full with water. Drop the first ink colour into the tray. making sure to cover the surface of the water.

Next drop any other colours into the water. You can manipulate the colours to create your design but remember to work quickly as the inks will dry after a couple of minutes.

When you are happy with the design and placement of the inks in the bath, gently bow the paper in the centre and lower it down into the water. This will help to avoid any air bubbles or misprints in the centre of the sheet. You can also lower the paper into the water at a 45-degree angle to ensure a good coverage of inks on the paper surface.

Blow or push away any excess ink from the surface of the water and remove the paper from the tray to reveal the pattern.

Set aside to dry. Whilst still just damp, place the marbled paper under a stack of heavy books to flatten it out as the water will leave some creases in the paper. Leave for 24 hours and it will be as flat as a pancake and ready for wrapping.

If you don't have a tray large enough for a full sheet of paper, you could just dip a section of the sheet to marble it.

Easter Eggs

For me Easter is Spring's Christmas with a lovely long weekend break and an opportunity to invite friends and family over for lunch. By the time Easter comes around, Spring is in full bloom and nature's colours are radiating. At this time of year I am most drawn to yellows, pastel hues and candy colours. Perhaps it's the summer sunshine to come or the association of little chicks and chocolates, but it definitely brings a lot of joy to my table.

I first started sharing marbling tutorials on my Instagram and back in Easter 2020 I showed my community how to create a simple but effective decoration using eggs for their Easter table. I am excited to share it with you here – eggs are inexpensive and look beautiful arranged in a bowl or hanging from a branch. This is also a great project to do with kids!

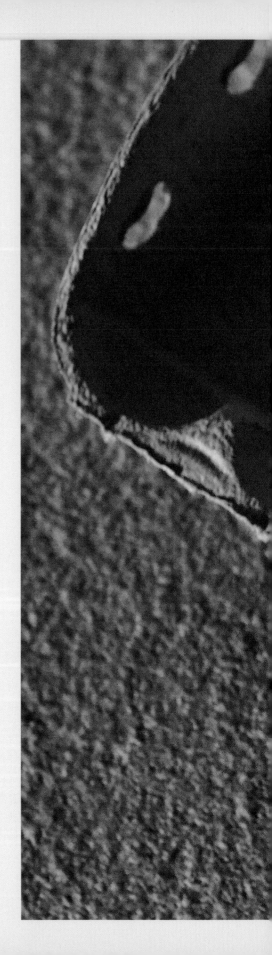

Hard-boiled (hard cooked) eggs will only last about a week, so if you want a longer lasting ornament it's best to blow the contents out.

Paint or spray your eggs with a clear matt or gloss varnish to protect the design over time.

You will need

Eggs – real, plastic or foam will all work for this project, I used eggs with ready-made loops for hanging ribbons

Deep bowl with enough room to submerge the eggs fully

Room temperature distilled water

Marbling inks suitable for ceramic and glass in 2–3 colours – I used Marabu Easy Marble solvent-based inks

Gloves

Stylus – cocktail sticks (toothpicks) or a wooden skewer

Drying space

Sewing needle and thread (optional)

2 beads (optional)

Thin ribbon to hang eggs with ready-made loops (optional)

Technique

We'll be using water marbling with ready-made inks for this project. Refer to pages 30–32 for the full method and page 140 for troubleshooting.

Preparation

Prepare the eggs by hard boiling them or alternatively use a large needle or cocktail stick (toothpicks) to pierce the top and bottom of the shell and carefully blow the egg out from one end to the other. Wash carefully by rinsing under the tap and leave to dry or pat dry with some kitchen towel.

How to

Fill your bowl two thirds full with water. Drop the first ink colour into the bowl, making sure to cover the surface of the water.

Next drop any other colours into the water. Don't use more that 2 or 3 or you'll over-saturate your work with colour. You can manipulate the colours to create your design but remember to work quickly as the inks will dry after a couple of minutes.

When you are happy with the design and placement of the inks in the bath, dip your egg into the bowl to submerge the area you'd like the ink to cover. You don't need to dip the whole egg – marbling looks great on just a section or you could mask off a specific shape.

Blow or push the remaining ink away from the surface before pulling the egg out of the bowl.

Leave to dry. The inks will be touch dry in around 15 minutes but leave for 24 hours to dry fully.

Once the eggs are completely dry, arrange them on your Easter table or in a bowl.

To hang blown eggs, thread a needle with ribbon or sewing cotton, insert it into the top hole in the egg, wiggle the needle through the egg carefully and through the bottom hole. Thread on a small bead and make a knot around it so it stays in place, then push the needle back through the egg and through the top hole again. Add another bead and knot the two threads to secure the bead and create a loop. You can then hang the eggs from a decorative branch.

Festive Baubles

I do love the festive season, it's one of my favourite times of year because it's an excuse to decorate our flat, be incredibly indulgent and really spoil friends and family. It's also a time of year when all I want to do is stay indoors and cosy up with some crafting. If it's not cutting out giant paper chains or snowflakes, it's making these marbled baubles. They're a gorgeous way to create festive ornaments that will be used year after year – or they can be kept out all year round. I usually spend the Sunday before the holiday season crafting baubles for friends and family as they make the perfect gift and there are always a few extra for me, too. Plus they're super speedy to make!

Other ideas

+ Velvet ribbon adds an extra luxurious feel to your ornaments – why not try contrasting colours.

+ Try some metallic inks to give your baubles some festive sparkle.

+ Paint or spray your ornaments with a clear matt or gloss varnish to protect the design over time.

+ Add some personalisation with a paint marker or initial stickers.

You will need

Rubbing alcohol

Lint-free cloth

Ceramic or glass baubles – both can be easily found online

Deep bottom bowl with enough room to submerge the ornament fully

Room-temperature distilled water

Marbling inks suitable for ceramic and glass in 2–3 colours – I used Marabu Easy Marble solvent-based inks

Gloves

Cocktail sticks (toothpicks) or a wooden skewer

Drying space

Ribbon or ric rac thin enough to fit through your chosen ornament

Technique

We'll be using water marbling with ready-made inks for this project. Refer to pages 30–32 for the full method and page 140 for troubleshooting.

Preparation

Gently clean the baubles with a cloth and rubbing alcohol before you begin, this will remove any dust and residue that could affect the marbling process.

How to

Fill your bowl two thirds full with water. Drop the first ink colour into the bowl, making sure to cover the surface of the water.

Next drop any other colours into the water, you can manipulate the colours as per your design but remember to work quickly as the inks will dry after a couple of minutes.

When you are happy with the design and placement of the inks in the water bath, dip your bauble into the bowl to submerge the area you'd like the ink to cover.

Blow or push the remaining ink away from the surface before pulling the bauble out of the bowl.

Leave to dry. The inks will be touch dry in around 15 minutes but leave for 24 hours to dry fully.

Once the baubles are completely dry I like to finish them off with a length of velvet ribbon or ric rac as this really elevates the ornament and they look lovely hanging up.

Two to three colours work best – any more and you'll over-saturate your work with colour.

As with the eggs on the previous pages, you don't need to dip the whole bauble into the marbling bath – try just a section or mask off a specific shape for a different effect.

Wooden Ornaments

As a true maximalist I need no excuse for a tasteful decorative object, and these wooden ornaments are beautiful works of art for your coffee table, shelfie – or even a friend. I picked these wooden toy blocks up from a charity store, gave them a splash of paint and voilà! Stack them up in sets of two, three or four.

Other ideas

+ This works brilliant on stones as well and is a lovely activity to do with kids.

+ Try dipping just a section of the block, or marble each side separately in a different pattern.

+ You could also try the nail polish marbling technique here (see pages 28–29).

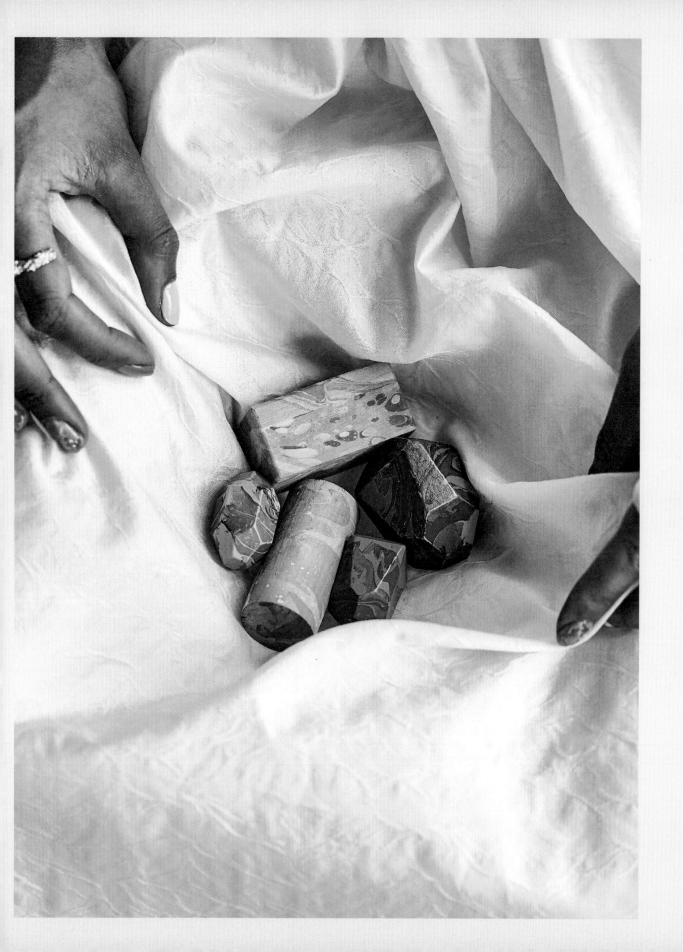

You will need

Fine sandpaper

Damp lint-free cloth

Rubbing alcohol

Wooden blocks, ideally untreated

Matt paint and paintbrush (optional)

Bowl or tray

Room-temperature distilled water

Marbling inks suitable for wood

Stylus

Gloves

Drying space

Scrap of paper or newsprint to clean the leftover ink

Spray clear matt varnish (optional)

Technique

We'll be using water marbling with ready-made inks for this project. Refer to pages 30–32 for the full method and page 140 for troubleshooting.

Preparation

Gently sand the blocks if coated and wipe clean of any dust. Use rubbing alcohol to remove any oily residue.

Paint the blocks if you would like to add a base layer of colour. I'd recommend a paler colour so as not to outshine the marbled pattern.

How to

Fill your tray or bowl two thirds full with water. Drop the first ink colour into the tray, making sure to cover the surface of the water.

Next drop any other colours into the water. You can manipulate the colours to create your design but remember to work quickly as the inks will dry after a couple of minutes.

When you are happy with the design and placement of the inks in the water bath, dip the block across the surface of the water to ensure it is coated with ink.

Blow or push away any excess ink from the surface of the water and remove the block from the tray.

Set aside to dry.

Clean away any leftover ink in the tray using a scrap of paper or newspaper, then repeat the process to marble all your remaining blocks.

You could spray them with clear varnish to protect the pattern.

Napkins

Once you've mastered the art of paper marbling it's time to move on to fabric. Whilst marbling on fabric is a little more time consuming it really is worth the effort – especially as you can create these stunning marbled napkins for your dining table. Using squares of cotton you can design a collection of beautiful tablelinen, or even reinvent some old napkins and give them a refresh with a marbled edge.

You will need

Marbling with fabric materials
and tools as listed on page 33

Cotton or linen napkins or fabric
squares approx. 40 x 40cm
(16 x 16in)

Sewing machine and matching
threads (optional)

Technique

We'll be using marbling with size to marble fabric in the
first part of this project. Refer to pages 33–39 for the full
method and page 140 for troubleshooting.

Preparation

When working with fabric marbling, always pre-wash your
fabrics to avoid any shrinkage later down the line and to
remove any residue that may still be on the fabric from the
manufacturing process. Leave the fabric to dry naturally.

You will need to prepare a marbling bath with size and
mordant your fabrics in advance of this project.

How to

Marble the napkins one by one following the marbling
with size technique.

If the napkins are too large to fit into the tray, try marbling
a section or marbling half and half at a time. I love the way
the print is really organic and random when working in this
way. Think about the way you will be folding the napkins
to help decide the placement of the print.

If marbling squares of cut fabric, finish the edges with
a zigzag stitch on the sewing machine or turn the seams
under to make a hem and sew with a straight stitch.

Wash on a cool cycle to remove any alum residue in
the fabric before using.

Place Settings

Setting the table with your guests' names is such a lovely way to make them feel really welcome at the dinner table. I love adding little details to make guests feel at home and it's also helpful for guests who might not know each other because a quick glance over will remind you of a name.

Other ideas

+ You could also use this technique to make matching menus. I recommend A5-size paper and marbling just the bottom half to leave space for the menu above.

+ Paint your guest's name onto a card place setting before marbling using masking fluid. This handy liquid dries translucent and can then be peeled away to reveal the name after the card is marbled. I've fond memories of using this at art school for a project all about peeling layers.

Harriet

You will need

Washi or frog tape

Tray large enough to hold the card

Room-temperature distilled water

Marbling inks suitable for paper

Stylus

Gloves

Plain or lightly coloured card place settings approx. 90cm (35½in) square – I usually buy ready-made but they're easy to cut yourself with a scalpel and cutting mat. To keep a premium feel, use 250–350gsm paper

Drying space

Scrap paper or newsprint to clean the leftover ink

Scalpel, cutting mat and metal ruler to cut place cards to size (optional)

Brush lettering pen or permanent marker to write names

Technique

We'll be using water marbling with ready-made inks for this project. Refer to pages 30–32 for the full method and page 140 for troubleshooting.

Preparation

Measure and cut the place cards to size. Score along the fold line with the back of the scalpel blade to create a clean fold line.

How to

Mask the centre of the place card with washi or frog tape before marbling. Once dry this can be easily peeled away to leave space to write your guest's name. Opt for a paler colour of marbling ink and a permanent pen if you'd like to marble the whole place setting.

Fill your tray two thirds full with water. Drop the first ink colour into the tray, making sure to cover the surface of the water.

Next drop any other colours into the water. You can manipulate the colours to create your design but remember to work quickly as the inks will dry after a couple of minutes.

When you are happy with the design and placement of the inks in the water bath, submerge the place cards into the tray to cover with marbling ink.

Blow or push away any excess ink from the surface of the water and remove the card from the tray. I recommend printing these one by one.

Set aside to dry.

Clean away the leftover ink in the tray using a scrap of paper or newspaper, then repeat the process to marble the remaining cards.

When fully dry, write a guest's name on each card and then fold the card in half.

Conclusion

Our marbling journey comes to an end! I hope this book has inspired you to try your hand at this endangered craft and embrace a more colourful and creative way of life. Apply the art of marbling to new and old objects in a contemporary way and add colour to anything from your tablescape to the way you think about gifting. Marbling is one of the most magical and mesmerising of crafts that you can lose yourself in, and it allows you to explore your creativity like no other. Whilst I know it can be rather challenging, it really does bear rewards and it is one of the most mindful ways to spend an afternoon, creating work that is so unique to you.

Now it's over to you and I'm so excited for you to continue your marbling journey; this is just the first part so keep spreading joy through colour and creativity.

Glossary

Alum This is short for aluminium potassium sulphate, which is a mordant used to treat paper and fabrics before marbling.

Carrageenan Also known as Irish moss, this is used to thicken the water bath for marbling – which is then called size.

Mordanting The process of treating paper and fabrics before marbling – it aids the inks in fixing to the surface of the material.

Paper stock The material from which paper is made.

Paper weight Paper is measured in weight (grams per square metre); the higher the gsm the thicker the paper will be.

Sampling The process of testing individual inks and marbling processes onto paper and fabric

Size This is the thickened water used to float inks onto when marbling.

References

heritagecrafts.org.uk/paper-marbling

Making Marbled Paper by Heather RJ Fletcher (2019, Fox Chapel Publishing)

The Whole Art of Marbling by CW Woolnough (2019, Six Penny Graphics)

The Practical Guide to Marbling Paper by Anne Chambers (1987, Thames & Hudson)

How to Marbleize Paper by Gabriele Grünebaum (2003, Dover Publications)

Marbling Techniques by Wendy Addison (2019, Echo Point Books)

Useful Suppliers

Fred Aldous fredaldous.co.uk

Cass Art cassart.co.uk

Jackson's jacksonsart.com

Great Art greatart.co.uk

George Weil georgeweil.com

Hobbycraft hobbycraft.co.uk

Baker Ross bakerross.co.uk

Cowling & Wilcox cowlingandwilcox.com

Jacquard For a wide range of marbling supplies, alum and carrageenan recipes; jacquardproducts.com

Troubleshooting

Colour

Stuck with colour? Have you used too many pigments and now you're in a bit of a muddle?

You might be having what I call a colour block. Colour can be overwhelming so take a break, grab a cup of tea and come back to it later with fresh eyes.

Often if the water bath has become muddy with inks and paints it can throw off your eye for colour so it is always worth cleaning out the water tray and starting afresh.

Choosing a tray with a white bottom is also helpful when you first start marbling because it will help you to see the colours more clearly.

Inks and paints

Marabu marbling inks or nail polish have gone gloopy?

It might be that you're working too slowly and you need to clean the bath and start again. Remember you only have a few minutes before the inks start to dry, it might seem like not enough time but it actually stops you overthinking it so you make quick decisions and really let go during the process.

Paints are sinking to the bottom of the tray?

Try adding some ox gall or Kodak Photo-Flo to help them float. Some colours need more than others so it is always a good idea to sample each colour before committing to the final project. It might be worth trying different brands of paint or inks as they do vary, too. I recommend Liquitex or the Golden brands as they work really nicely when marbling with size, and the Boku-Undo brand for Suminagashi.

Air bubbles in my paints?

Mixing your paints in advance will help with this because the air bubbles will slowly rise to the surface and pop. Use a cocktail stick (toothpick) or stylus to pop any that you see.

Embrace the bubbles – they often create rather happy accidents!

Size

My size is too thin?

You might have just added too much water; the consistency should feel like runny honey and be thick enough to hold the inks on the surface. If you have added too much water you will need to remix your size again, the more meticulous the better, and refer to the manufacturer's recipes where possible.

My size is too thick?

Gradually add more water if the size feels too thick, measure it carefully and make notes for next time. Leave it for a few hours to settle again before marbling.

Lots of air bubbles?

Leave the size overnight to avoid this, they will gradually float to the surface and pop. Use a stylus or cocktail stick (toothpick) to burst any bubbles you might see.

Mordanting

I followed the process for mordanting but the ink is washing off my paper

Some papers will work better than others, make sure to choose an uncoated natural paper stock. Anything with a slight gloss or waxy finish won't work and inks will wash off.

Try mordanting the paper again and following the manufacturer's recipes.

I'd recommend mordanting the paper the day before you marble it because it will only last a couple of days.

My fabric doesn't seem to be mordanted properly, it's not taking the inks

Again you might need to repeat the mordanting process following the manufacturer's guidelines.

Have you pre-washed your fabric? It may be that you need to pre-wash it again as it may have some residue on the surface that is affecting the mordanting process.

Marbling works best on 100% natural fabrics, so make sure you are working with natural materials where possible or with a low percentage of man-made fibres. Always sample your fabric first.

My paper hasn't printed completely

This may be due to poor mordanting, so repeat the process.

Or it could be the way you place the paper into the surface of the marbling bath. Practise with your samples by placing the paper in at a 45-degree angle or hold the sheet of paper from opposite corner to corner and gently bow the centre of the paper into the water first before letting the edges go. Practice makes perfect so don't worry if you haven't got it the first time.

There are lines or gaps in my print

These are hesitation lines, so try to place the material more decisively into the marbling bath – just go for it! You can always dip it again once it is dry.

My objects aren't printing properly

This may be due to poor mordanting or cleaning. Clean objects before marbling using some rubbing alcohol and a soft cloth to remove any dirt, dust or residue that might prevent the ink from sticking.

Thanks

There are just so many wonderful humans and special people in my life to thank, those of you that helped me to bring this book to life – you know who you are.

The biggest thank you of all must go to my incredible husband and love of my life Zack, your endless support and encouragement know no bounds and this book is as much yours as mine. Thank you for always being there to listen to my wild ideas, spur me on, man the camera so brilliantly and run back and forth to the studio for forgotten props and tools! I'm so lucky to share my world with such a kind, generous and talented man.

To my editor Harriet, this book wouldn't be real without you and I can't thank you enough for seeing the magic in marbling and bringing a dream come true project to life, as well as championing an endangered craft. This book couldn't be more me if it tried! Thank you also for your immense patience, kindness and support in creating this book over a pretty bonkers time. Emily and Ore, it has been a joy to work with such a talented dream team. Emily, your amazing design skills and knack for finding just the right location house have brought my vision to life and I am just so over the moon to see it all come together. It's a real book! To lovely Kristen Perers and her assistant Sophie for turning my marbled projects into such exquisite images that will be treasured forever. It has been an honour and dream come true to work with you having been a fan girl of your work for such a long time. Thank you for having

us in your beautiful space, The Flower Factory is as stunning as it looks. To Clare Love whose flowers in this book will bring endless joy, you nailed the colour brief, thank you! To Arevik the pink baker whose cakes I was determined to get into one of my tablescapes. Thank you for making the perfect heart-shaped cake for the gal who loves hearts!

To my manager and friend Harry, thank you for being there to support me and letting me get on with things my way! You have helped me know my worth and for that I will be forever grateful. Thank you for always being my cheerleader and having the patience of a saint!

To my parents – without their endless hard work, dedication to my sisters and I, and all round lust for the good things in life I wouldn't be the person I am today. To my mum especially for inspiring me to craft and make things from such an early age, it was true love. Thank you for always encouraging my creativity. My heritage plays a huge part in this book and my love of colour and eye for it have certainly come from somewhere, I feel so lucky to be able to share it and inspire so many more people with this book.

Last but not least to all the suppliers that supported me in the making of this book; Falcon Enamelware you do make the very best marbling vessels, Pfaff your sewing machines are like no other, Clare Love Blooms for all the flowers, Arevik @thepinkcooker for the most good looking cake and The Stem for the most stunning plants that really do brighten up my studio daily.

Managing Director Sarah Lavelle
Senior Commissioning Editor Harriet Butt
Assistant Editor Oreolu Grillo
Copy Editor Marie Clayton
Proofreader Gillian Haslam
Art Director + Designer Emily Lapworth
Photographer Kristin Perers
Photographer's Assistant Sophie Bronze
Stylist Milly Bruce
Make-up Artist Laura Anne
Head of Production Stephen Lang
Production Controller Nikolaus Ginelli

Published in 2022 by Quadrille,
an imprint of Hardie Grant Publishing

Quadrille
52–54 Southwark Street
London SE1 1UN
quadrille.com

Cataloguing in Publication Data: a catalogue record
for this book is available from the British Library.

text © Zeena Shah 2022
photography © Kristin Perers 2022
design © Quadrille 2022

ISBN 978 1 78713 840 7

Printed in China

Printed using soy inks

FSC
www.fsc.org

MIX
Paper from
responsible sources
FSC™ C020056